Foreword by Sir Ric

THE COURAGE MAP

13 PRINCIPLES TO LIVING BOLDLY

FRANZISKA ISELI

ISBN: 978-1-63161-081-3

Published by TCK Publishing
www.TCKpublishing.com

TCK PUBLISHING.COM

Dear Courage,

I love hanging out with you. You are fun. You help me evolve. And you challenge me to become a better human.

You show me that, when someone tells me something is impossible, I can choose not to believe it. You cheer me on and allow me to live a life filled with infinite magical moments.

You push my boundaries. At times you take my breath away, and at times you make me a little nervous.

Thanks to you, I will look back on my life with a big smile and a heart filled with gratitude, knowing that I stayed true to myself and lived my life courageously, without regrets.

I am forever grateful for you. Thank you for all that you have taught me and continue to teach me!

I love you.
Franziska

TABLE OF CONTENTS

FOREWORD BY SIR RICHARD BRANSON

I've always had a love for adventure, and I've been blessed to share many of them with my family and friends. So when Franziska told me about her motorbike journey along the Silk Road, I was intrigued.

Every day I see people doing great things in the world. What do they have in common? The courage to go after their dreams and make a positive impact. Franziska's book shows how that message can support you in running your life and business based on courage, love, and kindness instead of fear.

I may not be the bravest or smartest person, but I dream big, surround myself with brilliant people, and take bold risks. The courage to dare has led me on the journey of a lifetime. Courage enabled me to make the right decisions, whether that was to protest against the Vietnam War as a teenager, or to push boundaries by starting businesses like Virgin Galactic.

Courage is not the absence of fear. Courage is feeling fear and doing it anyway. Courage is not about being reckless, it's about taking calculated risks. Courage enables you to take action instead of waiting for the confidence to do so.

What did I know about running a magazine when I was a teenager? Could I really manage a global record label? What on earth was a hippie like me doing starting an airline? Was I crazy trying to fly a balloon around the world, or build a commercial spaceline? I've always believed in challenging myself, and I think we all do our best work when we take chances and stretch ourselves.

That doesn't mean it isn't scary. But with adventurers like Franziska to guide the way, and tools like this book, we can all find the courage to take a chance and be courageous.

Screw it, just do it!

Richard

INTRODUCTION

Courage is the source of a meaningful and fulfilling human existence. Courage is the instigator of life's greatest experiences, those memorable moments that have the ability to change the course of your life for the better. Courage is your best ally in helping you live your life fully. Courage supports you as you face meaningful challenges in life, make better decisions, and stay true to yourself when you're tempted to give in.

Best of all, courage is a skill that anyone can learn. This book will show you how to make courage your superpower no matter where you're at, and regardless of how the past has shaped your life.

In early 2018 I had the "best worst idea": to ride a motorbike from Switzerland, my home country, along the Silk Road and into Asia. I wanted to follow the steps of explorer Marco Polo, an Italian merchant and writer famous for his travels in the thirteenth century.

Since I felt called to challenge myself, I decided to make this journey a solo trip. I was confident riding motorbikes, but I didn't know how to fix one, let alone change a tire on the Afghan border or make it through waist-deep, freezing rivers. Still, I thought I'd figure it out on my own along the twelve-thousand-kilometer journey. I may have been a bit delusional.

A few weeks after I decided to embark on this adventure, I met Mike Cline at a social entrepreneurship conference in the Bahamas. Over dinner, Mike mentioned something about riding motorbikes, so I told him about my upcoming Silk Road journey. His eyes widened. He had wanted to do this same trip for over a decade. "Would you be open to having a road buddy?" he asked.

At first I hesitated, but on second thought I realized that having a travel partner in some of the countries I was planning to visit would be a good idea—especially one who knows how to fix bikes and read maps! Mike saved my butt more than once on that trip.

In July 2018, Mike and I met up at my mom's house in Switzerland, and from there, we hit the road.

I had been sharing my thoughts on courage in speeches for a while, but it wasn't until that motorbike journey that I realized I had to write this book. Spending so much time in my helmet—sometimes eight to ten hours per day—gave me a lot of time to reflect and think deeply about the principles of courage I'm about to share with you.

This book will help you understand where your fears come from, how to reclaim control of your life, and how to live a courageous life—a life you love and are proud to call your own.

WHY COURAGE MATTERS

Courage is one of the most powerful forces you can use to shape your life. It allows you to stay true to yourself, lead by example, make a positive impact, and live without regrets. Courage is the underlying force that allows you to make small and big changes, both personally and professionally.

Everyone has plenty of ideas and dreams to live an exceptional life. What some of us lack is the courage to turn those ideas into reality and pursue our dreams with gusto.

EXPAND YOUR COURAGE BOUNDARIES

The purpose of this book is to show you how you can expand your courage boundaries in every area of life.

Your courage boundaries, or the borders of your comfort zone, define the level of risk or uncertainty you are comfortable with. Risks always have potential costs, but they also come with potential rewards. As we get older, we tend to allow our courage boundaries to shrink as we begin to avoid potentially painful and risky things. But as your boundaries shrink, so do your possibilities. The good news is that your boundaries are flexible, and you can intentionally develop the courage you need to start in a whole new direction and reap the rewards of a fulfilling life.

As you design your Courage Map and apply the principles explained throughout this book, you will expand your boundaries. You'll feel more courageous as you begin to identify new opportunities and take new actions. You'll be able to do things you used to think were impossible for you. You will feel uncomfortable at times, but remember: that's just part of the process! That uncomfortable feeling simply means that you are making progress.

To support you on this road trip, I've designed a journal so you can draw your own Courage Map and jot down ideas, insights, and action steps along the way. You can download it at franziskaiseli.com/thecouragemap

As you build even more courage and explore your boundaries, trust in the process. You will come across many delightful surprises, as well as some roadblocks while you explore exciting, uncharted territories. Embrace your journey and remind yourself to keep chasing your wildest dreams.

Developing more courage is an ongoing process, not a one-time procedure. So keep coming back to your Courage Map and notes whenever you feel it's time for a tune-up.

You might find that random thoughts or observations related to these courage principles pop up throughout the day. I suggest you write these thoughts down, unedited. You will start to see subtle shifts and significant changes as you become more aware of your patterns of thought, behavior, and feeling while going through this book.

You could also use your Courage Map as your one-year evolutionary plan, where you adopt one new principle per month. Or, you might choose to speed up your journey. You decide! It's your adventure.

WHAT IS COURAGE?

Courage is not about being fearless; it's about making brave decisions despite fear. Courage is a skill. It's the ability to overcome your habitual responses to fear, and to react consciously in your best interest and the interests of others. Courageous people stay true to themselves, take risks, face challenges head-on, and lead by example.

Courage gives you the ability to confront what frightens you. You can see it in a timid child talking to his peers on the playground despite his shyness, a pioneer discovering new territories despite the risks, a firefighter running into a burning house to save people despite the likelihood of getting injured, or a best friend giving a speech at your birthday party despite her fear of public speaking.

Courage is not about being reckless. Recklessness is driving on the wrong side of the road in the path of oncoming traffic, or jumping off a cliff without knowing the depth of the water below. Recklessness is about taking risks that aren't worth it—irresponsible risks. Courage is about taking risks that are so worth it—worthwhile risks.

Courage is not about proving yourself to anyone; it's about being your true self and living life without regrets.

Courage will allow you to:

- say yes even when the odds are against you.
- say no, even when it's easier to say yes.
- live with an open heart.
- stand up for your beliefs even when it's uncomfortable.
- face difficult conversations.
- love unconditionally.
- make big decisions.
- embark on new adventures.
- pursue goals that others say are impossible.
- trust yourself fully.

Courage is taking action in the face of fear. You can choose to either dance with fear gracefully, or let her step all over your feet. I say, let's dance!

4 THINGS COURAGEOUS PEOPLE DO

As you navigate through this book, you will learn to adopt four key behaviors that will lead you to a life of courage.

1. Stay true to yourself

Courageous people know their truth and stand up for what they believe in, even if it's easier to back down. They have very strong values and a belief system that supports them as they stand in their truth with conviction.

They are not afraid to swim against the current or challenge conventional thinking, and they are committed to constantly learning, evolving, and improving in every area of life.

2. Take more risks

Courageous people take more risks in order to make a bigger impact and live a better life. They understand that things might not always work out the way they expect, but they won't settle for the status quo without at least trying to make a change for the better. They step out of their comfort zones and embrace the unknown for the sake of growth. They take bold leaps in life with faith, despite all their fears and doubts.

3. Face difficulties head on

Courageous people have an ability to boldly confront problems, situations, and challenges. They don't run from problems. Instead, they face challenging situations head-on for the benefit of everyone involved. They do so with truth, respect, and integrity.

4. Lead by example

Courageous people lead by example. They lead with courage, kindness, and empathy. They are unattached to their fears, doubts, and what other people might think about them.

They are committed to integrity and they back up their words with actions. They know the difference between right and wrong and stand up to injustice with kindness. They take action and inspire others to step up with courage too.

ASK QUESTIONS

Courage not only helps you stay true to yourself, take more risks, face challenging situations, and lead with impact, but it also helps you to free yourself from limiting social rules (and your own made-up rules too!).

Don't buy into non-sensical societal rules that can hold you back on your journey to courage.

I have this pet peeve about rules that don't make sense. There are so many societal rules that are useless. Here are some that come to mind. I'm sure you can think of many more!

- Why do you have to park your car facing a specific direction along the street (in Australia at least)?
- Why is it considered weird to eat pizza for breakfast or cereal for dinner?
- Why is unconditional love so difficult?
- Why is it considered rude to wear a hat at the dinner table?
- Why do guys not wear skirts (well, at least not many)?
- Why would it be frowned upon to go to work in a bathrobe? (Oh, how I love my bathrobe!)
- Why is it considered weird to skip down the street unless you're a child?
- Why is nose-picking not cool?
- Why do we need to look into each other's eyes when toasting? (I actually love this one! And I make sure to never miss eye contact when toasting because in Switzerland, we say that you'll have seven years of bad sex if you don't. You're welcome!)

Instead of automatically accepting everything that society, family, colleagues, or so-called experts say, question things that don't make sense to you.

My mom recounts a story when I came home from school one day and asked her if I could go see my best friend, Flawia. She said no. That didn't make any sense to me because I couldn't think of a reason why she would say no. I had done all my homework and wasn't grounded, so I asked pragmatically, "Um, Mom, do you have a reason why I'm not allowed to go?"

My mom paused and thought for a minute. "Actually, no, I don't have a reason—other than me having a bad day and being grumpy."

I'm glad I asked the question, because that small act of courage made a big difference, and I was able to spend time with my best friend that day because of it. Sometimes one simple question can sometimes turn an average moment into a joyful one.

You don't need to accept everything that people tell you or that others expect you to do. Have the courage to question anything that doesn't make sense to you. And do so with love.

A lot of rules and barriers are self-imposed. Some stem from beliefs you've inherited from your parents and friends, and some come from your own experiences. Don't just accept the world the way it is or the way you think things are. Have the courage to ask more questions and figure things out for yourself.

THE QUESTION THAT CHANGED EVERYTHING

I was sitting on the floor eating scrambled eggs on toast after a long surf when my phone rang. I heard my brother's voice. That phone call changed the way I looked at life forever. Our father, who was a young fifty-eight, had had a heart attack and passed away unexpectedly. I can't describe the shock and sadness I felt, even all these years later.

One question kept coming back to me throughout that time, and it's a question I still ask myself now: "Would I be happy with my life if I died right now?"

Courage is a skill. No matter how little or how much courage you have now, you can always find more. You can make a conscious effort to expand your courage boundaries.

If the answer is yes, I keep doing what I'm doing. If the answer is no, I know I need to change something. This one question has led me to take courageous action at times when it would have been easier to stay comfortable. It's a great question to ask yourself throughout your life. Let your answer guide your decisions.

Becoming aware of my own mortality and witnessing how quickly life can change has helped me to actively choose the way I live instead of being driven by fear. This awareness has helped me to give life my all and make courageous decisions despite my fears.

Don't embark on this voyage to living more boldly for me, your partner, your mother, or your brother. Do it for you.

HOW COURAGE SHAPED MY LIFE

Courage has not only helped me stay true to myself in my personal life, but it has also allowed me to make an impact through entrepreneurship by building businesses and teams from a place of courage, creating positive ripple effects. It has been a challenging endeavor at times, and I've made more mistakes than I can count. However, using entrepreneurship to solve meaningful problems has been, and still is, a worthwhile challenge and important mission for me.

After earning my master's degrees in political science and marketing, I started my corporate career as an advertising strategist. I felt safe with my regular paycheck, but it was way too predictable for me. I had a yearning to use my skills to make a bigger impact. Growing up in Switzerland, however, I had been ingrained with conformist values and was taught that "you shouldn't leave the security of a high-flying career."

So, it took courage for me to quit my job and start a new business. Today, Basic Bananas is a marketing mentorship organization that leads marketing trainings for small to medium-sized business owners around the world. After I started that first business, I founded other companies and invested in projects that fuel my heart and make a positive impact.

Oceanlovers is one of those projects. I was sitting in the ocean on a hot summer night in Sydney when I had an epiphany about ocean conservation. More and more plastics are piling up on once pristine beaches, water temperatures are rising, and coral and sea life are dying. I knew I had to do something about this issue.

How can we motivate more people to care? By building an attractive brand that moves minds and hearts.

A few months later a new business was born with a big purpose: to "inspire and motivate the masses to save our oceans." Oceanlovers encourages people to pick up trash from our beaches by providing a platform with sustainable, ocean-inspired products. We were one of the first businesses to create surf suits made from plastic bottles and fishing lines. It took courage to launch—we had no idea whether people would be interested in what we were offering. Luckily, people all over the world love our mission and want to be part of it!

In our brand consultancy The Business Hood, we are often challenged to be brave enough to say no to certain clients or projects that don't align with our values and mission. And we don't always get it right.

There were so many moments over the past decade that scared me and made my heart beat faster. Sometimes I felt like I had no idea what I was doing (and I still feel that way often). In those moments, I must remember to trust myself and do the right thing, no matter how scary or difficult that is. And of course I've made many mistakes, all of which have helped me to learn, grow, and evolve.

When you step into courage, opportunities will come to you. But obstacles will show up as well, so you must be able to navigate roadblocks and setbacks without letting fear stop you. If you live courageously, you will die without regrets, because you will have given life everything you've got.

BUT WHAT ABOUT FEAR?

To understand courage, we need to understand fear.

Let's look at fear as a character so we can understand her better. Imagine fear as a freaky-looking alien: When you look at her from afar, she's intimidating. But the more you become familiar with her, the less frightening she will seem.

Fear functions similarly to any other emotion. If you allow it to pass through you, rather than fighting it or running from it, it will eventually dissipate. So instead of heading for the hills when you see fear rear her ugly head, stand still and face her. Feel her. Allow her to move in on you. When you do that, she will move past you. In fact, most of the time, all she was doing was trying to keep you safe!

What's on the other side of fear? What happens when you have the courage to get past your fears? Freedom.

On your path between fear and freedom, you'll experience all kinds of feelings: confusion, doubt, lack of self-worth, and anything in between. But then you reach freedom, this incredibly delicious feeling of limitlessness, curiosity, and clarity.

Just like with anything in life, you can get better at stepping through fear. It's a practice: the more you do it, the easier it gets. Getting closer to freedom is like shedding the unnecessary layers that have been weighing you down.

The goal is not to avoid fear; the goal is to be able to navigate through it with grace and ease, to see it as a teacher. You can learn to feel safe and comfortable despite the fear.

FEAR IS SAFE

Fear is one of the safest places you can ever find yourself in. Fear holds you in your position; she doesn't want you to fail. She wants you to stay safe. She wants to protect you.

The trouble with fear, however, is that sometimes she protects you even when you don't need to be protected. She can't distinguish between when you need to be kept safe and when you need to be pushed out of your comfort zone.

Fear will try to keep you safe from:

- opening your heart and loving wildly
- taking a leap of faith
- letting go of someone
- saying yes to something new
- trusting yourself
- paddling into a big wave
- leaving a safe job
- wearing something a little bit out of your comfort zone
- taking a stance for what you believe in
- standing up for a loved one
- being vulnerable

These are all very different scenarios, but they all have one thing in common: each involves a certain level of risk. You could make a mistake and fail. Yet having the courage to make mistakes and fail forward—to use the mistakes as stepping-stones—will allow you to make progress and live your richest life. Failures are lessons that can lead you to evolve and reach new heights.

A close friend recently asked me, "What if you regret a brave decision? What if you realize you've made the 'wrong' decision?"

It's not a question of if you mess up; it's a question of when. Because we all make mistakes. Instead of feeling regret, take it as a great chance to course-correct. Acknowledge yourself for being brave enough to take a step toward what you really want. Failure is a great opportunity to evolve and adjust your life's path, rather than staying stuck in the same place.

This may sound "woo woo" to you, but I believe the universe always has a way of making things work out. Sometimes it takes a little longer than you may like, and sometimes the way things work out don't make sense until you look back on them years later.

Do you remember a moment when you did something that really scared you? Or maybe you made a mistake, and then later realized that everything was still OK or even better? Me too! Sometimes your "big failures" turn out to be big blessings. By understanding this and keeping a balanced perspective on your failures, you'll be able to take more risks in life, knowing that things will work out for you one way or another.

Being courageous in the face of fear helps you go places most people won't dare to go.

THE FEAR PRISON

Fear can become a prison if you ignore her or run away from her.

It's crucial that you remain aware of fear so that she doesn't drive your behavior, unconsciously or consciously. Don't allow her to dominate your daily experiences. Don't become a prisoner. Stay aware of your emotions, be OK with feeling fear, and then make the right choice about how you want to react to her.

One strategy I've discovered that stops fear from pulling me into an emotional prison is journaling. When fear is clouding my mind, then I'm at risk of getting stuck or procrastinating. So, if I have to make a decision or take action on something that frightens me, I turn to my notebook.

I write down my thoughts, whatever comes out. I journal every day until I regain clarity and am ready to take courageous action in line with my true self. This process helps me regain control of my life so fear can't stop me from living boldly. Sometimes that process takes a few days, sometimes a lot longer.

Maybe journaling will work for you too. You might find writing a letter to a loved one works better, or that discussing your fears with a friend does wonders. Everyone has slightly different ways to process emotions and find clarity, so honor what works for you.

Fear keeps us safe. She helps us stay alive. Fear is something to be grateful for, but don't let her put you in a prison.

Living courageously means taking the leap despite your fear!

YOUR COURAGE MAP

In this book, you will be designing your very own Courage Map for living boldly, going after your wildest dreams, and leaving your mark on the world.

A map is a drawing or representation of an area with a view from above. Your Courage Map is your very own drawing and view from above that will help you to think and act in ways that will expand your courage boundaries. It's your guide to a bold life.

Your map might look very different than someone else's. You choose how you want to travel, which mountains you want to climb, which oceans you want to cross, what tunes you want to listen to, where you want to stop, and who you want to travel with. This is your map and your journey into courage.

Make sure to download your free *The Courage Map* journal here: franziskaiseli.com/thecouragemap

THE JOURNEY AHEAD

In this book, you will find thirteen principles that will help you to develop your courage and expand your boundaries. The purpose of each principle is to support you as you make bolder decisions and live a life you can look back on without regrets. These principles are the compass that will guide you on this journey.

TRAVEL TUNES

What's a great road trip without music? Music has an incredible ability to enhance any journey. At the end of each principle you will find a few "travel tunes" to help you apply the principle to your everyday life. They are sets of positive beliefs or affirmations that you can repeat to yourself to make each principle a habit.

Just like your favorite travel tunes you play on repeat while road tripping, your courage-promoting travel tunes will gradually become a part of you.

PIT STOPS

Pit stops are just as important as the journey itself. Following the principles and the travel tunes, there will be an invitation to refuel and put the principle to work with fun challenges, action steps, and practical exercises.

TRAVEL JOURNAL

At the end of each principle, you will find a few questions to ponder. Pause and take some time to think about how you can incorporate each principle into your life.

Some principles will be easier to apply than others, and some will resonate with you more than others. And some you may already be applying in your life. By diving even deeper into these principles, you'll be able to turn your courage up a few extra notches.

Thank you for choosing to live boldly! The world needs your courage!

THE END

Often when you embark on a journey, you know the destination you are aiming for. You might not always know how you will get there, but you usually start with the end in mind.

Let's take a few minutes to think about where you would like to end up on your journey with courage. What kind of person do you want to become? What would be a great destination for you to reach as you design your Courage Map?

Grab your notebook and write down your thoughts about the following questions:

- What does living courageously mean to you? What does living boldly look like for you?
- When do you feel most courageous?
- In which areas of your life would you like to be more courageous?

- What impact would living boldly have on you and those around you?
- What are you most afraid of?
- How has fear held you back in life?
- What decisions would you make and what actions would you take if you had all the courage you needed?

Once you've thought about these questions, pay attention to your current courage boundaries and then observe your evolution as you move through this book. You'll be surprised at how just a few small adjustments can make a huge difference.

Courage is a skill. No matter how little or how much courage you have now, you can always find more. You can make a conscious effort to expand your courage boundaries.

FOR YOU

This book is for you if you want to be more courageous. It's for you if you have a desire to give life your best shot. It's for you if you want to live your truth. And it's especially for you if you want to create ripple effects while leading by example and inspiring others to lead courageous lives too.

The world needs your superpowers! Imagine a planet where more and more people stop sleepwalking through their days and instead have the courage to stand up for their principles, speak up, do what's right, create, innovate, and honor themselves and others without judgment.

COURAGE - < SKILL
BOUNDARIES "COURAGE MAP"

1- STAY AUTHENTIC
2- TAKE RISKS
3- FACE IT HEAD ON
4- Lead by example
4.5- ASK QUESTIONS

FEAR- keeps you
1- SAFE -
2- PRISON - entrapped

AFTER FEAR IS FREEDOM
JOURNEY TO GET THROUGH IT

THE 13 PRINCIPLES TO LIVING BOLDLY

PRINCIPLE 1: STORIES

Human beings naturally find meaning in all kinds of experiences. It's how we make sense of the world. We turn every experience we have into a story, and our stories give meaning to our human existence. Stories are what define us as humans. As we go through life, we unconsciously add our very own interpretation or meaning to the experiences we live—either to our detriment or to our advantage.

The stories you tell yourself and others create a lens through which you see the world, and this perspective will determine whether you act out of fear or courage. Your stories determine how courageously you will live. And because you are the author of your own stories, you can rewrite the ones that don't serve you.

WHO AM I WITHOUT MY STORIES?

"Every parent messes up their children!" one of my friends exclaimed. It made me laugh.

It also made me think. Maybe she was right—we are all a little bit messed up. But it's not that our parents consciously decided to damage our internal software; it's that we unconsciously allow our software to be altered through the meanings we give our experiences.

"We tell ourselves stories in order to live."
—Joan Didion

Each story can be crafted in a way that either helps you to be more courageous, or pushes you to live in fear. It is a choice, although often an unconscious one. Every moment is an opportunity for you to write a new story. Stories are like maps: they help you see and understand the incredibly complex world in a much simpler way. Stories shape your belief systems.

Stories may be at the origin of your character formation, but they are not your essence.

Stories are the layers you add to your being, just like putting on layers of clothes as summer turns into winter. Your winter clothes are there to keep you warm, to protect you from the cold. The same goes with stories.

Some clothes make you feel attractive, and some make you feel uncomfortable. Stories do the same. Some empower you, while others make you feel miserable and hold you back from living boldly. For example, a story that makes you believe you can't trust others will lead you to meet new people with distrust. On the other hand, a story that tells you people generally mean well will cause you to feel more relaxed and intuitive around strangers.

As you grow older, you keep adding layers to your core being. That's why you often hear people say, "I just don't know who I am anymore; I feel lost." Disempowering stories that create limiting beliefs have been piled up one atop another until you've forgotten who you really are and what really matters to you. Some of your stories can quash courage and lead you to live in fear, while others encourage you to step up. The only way to get back to your true self is by shedding or rewriting the stories that don't serve you any longer.

I was in second grade when, during one of our morning breaks, I ducked into the bathroom. When I tried to unlock the stall door, it wouldn't open. I was locked in! I heard the break bell ring outside, and fear bubbled up inside me. The other kids all headed back to class, and I was left alone. I frantically banged on the door hoping someone would hear me, but no luck. After a few harrowing minutes, my teacher and most of my class (including the boys) were standing in the bathroom trying to "save" me.

I was so embarrassed as I walked out of the stall, teary-eyed with my head hanging low. I told myself the story that locking the door in public bathrooms isn't safe. For many years after that, I would often leave the bathroom door unlocked.

I was recently enjoying a margarita at a Mexican restaurant in San Francisco with some of my friends when I had to go to the bathroom. After not returning for ten minutes, my friends started to wonder what was going on. Well, I couldn't open the locked door! I instantly hit the panic button and climbed over the top of the door instead.

The stories you tell yourself are powerful. They can make you live with irrational fears for years to come, or they can enable you to act from a place of calm courage. You are the author of your own stories.

THE STORIES WE CHOOSE

As I was working on this book, I paid special attention to my own thoughts and tried to dissect my behaviors in order to share the lessons with you. One thing that I kept asking myself was: "Do I have daddy issues because I never heard my dad say the words 'I love you?'" I looked back into my childhood memories to see which disempowering stories I made up when I was a child.

Growing up, I don't ever remember my dad telling me that he loved me. Does that mean that he didn't love me? Or that I am not lovable? It means exactly what I decide it means, because I am the author of my own stories.

What I discovered is that instead of concluding that my dad's lack of expression meant he didn't love me, it meant that he just wasn't very good at putting feelings into words. My dad grew up in difficult circumstances, and he probably never learned how to express love verbally. I also chose to believe that actions are more important than words (something I still believe wholeheartedly now).

Am I living in denial so I can pretend to be happy with a "better" story? I don't think so—but even if I am, an experience only has the meaning you choose to give it! You are the author of your stories. The true measure of a personal story's impact isn't necessarily how accurate it is, but how valuable it is. Does it fill you with courage and help you become a better person? Or does it make you resentful, depressed, and misable?

There is one particular experience with my dad that I carry deep in my heart, one I have chosen to remember and cherish, instead of hanging on to some of the less amazing ones.

I was about ten years old. The horse stable where I took riding lessons was running a show-jumping competition on a Saturday afternoon. Being the youngest and most inexperienced rider, I was both excited and very nervous.

Since I didn't own my own horse, my teacher let me use one of his: Risiko, a brown-coated, gentle giant. As Saturday morning approached, I could hardly contain my excitement and nerves. I woke up early and put on my white riding pants and the black blazer I had borrowed from a friend. My mom and dad drove me to the school. Yes! My dad came to see me!

I walked the show-jumping ground with my fellow competitors to memorize the course and sequence of obstacles so we would remember which way to guide our horses in the competition. I became more nervous by the minute.

Risiko and I rode in front of the judges' desk and waited for the bell. I pressed my heels into Risiko's side and he started to gallop toward the first obstacle. Everything went well until we were approaching the fourth obstacle—a wide ditch. We approached the ditch at full speed. Risiko changed his mind at the last minute and came to a full stop in front of it. I went flying over his head and hit the ground hard.

Amazingly, I wasn't hurt. I got up, dusted off my now-stained pants, adjusted my helmet, and walked over to Risiko. He looked at me with his big, brown, gentle eyes. I grabbed his reins, jumped back on, and we attempted obstacle four again.

This time Risko did jump and we finished the rest of the course.

One moment from this day will stick with me forever: As I picked myself up off the ground, I looked over to my parents standing by the fence. I saw my dad with tears in his eyes. Not because I fell down and finished last in the competition, but because he was proud that I got back up.

I had never seen my dad cry before. It was such a precious moment, and one I will remember for the rest of my life. I decided to believe that my dad loved me and that he was proud of his daughter, even when he couldn't express himself verbally. It's a story that has supported me and it fills my heart to this day.

I could have picked a different meaning for that moment. If I had chosen to believe that I am not loved, I might have unconsciously messed up all my adult relationships with men (some of which I certainly have). Or, I could have believed that I'm not a good horse rider and stopped showing up at competitions. Or that it's easier to stay safe and never try anything out of my comfort zone because when I did, I fell flat on my face.

Which stories are you choosing to keep? Which ones are empowering you to be courageous? Which ones are holding you back? Which ones are encouraging you to live fully?

You always have a choice.

You only need to listen to your friends around a dinner table to realize how many are holding on to stories that don't serve them. For example, one of my friends had a really bad relationship experience and her story of that relationship tells her she is not worthy. The fear of unworthiness is driving her behavior. When she meets a man she likes, she feels fear and thinks that she doesn't deserve his love and respect. A more serving story she could adopt is that the last relationship was not meant to work out because there is something much greater waiting for her.

So why can it be so challenging to recognize and drop the stories that are holding you back from living the life you want?

You hold on to stories, no matter how disempowering or empowering they are, because they fill a certain need—maybe a need for attention or significance, to be heard, to belong, or to be loved.

If a story is serving one of your needs, it is less likely you will change it. Does that mean you are stuck with it for life? Nope! You just have to find another story to replace the old one—one that empowers you to live boldly.

Please be gentle with yourself as you reexamine your own stories. Some experiences and stories are a lot harder and take longer to kick than others. You are not alone on this journey

You've got this!

Control your narrative

TOO MUCH DRAMA

Let's talk a little bit about a human phenomenon that is holding so many people back from stepping up, owning their results, and living their truth boldly: drama. By drama I'm not referring to a play or movie, but the irrational human behavior of overreacting or making something out to be bigger than it is.

What causes people to create drama? What is the purpose of drama? Why are some people more prone to drama than others?

Drama is driven by the stories you tell yourself. Disempowering stories are the perfect breeding ground for drama. Without a story, drama can't exist. Getting upset with someone over something seemingly meaningless happens because of the stories you tell yourself. It's a behavior rooted in fear.

For some people, it may seem easier to act out in drama than to rewrite their stories. However, once you are aware of your patterns, you can choose a different behavior.

Drama is often a call for someone's attention. Drama doesn't work when you're alone; it requires company. If the call is not answered, drama will eventually disappear. You need more than one person involved for drama to flourish or get out of hand.

How do you respond when others create unnecessary drama? Do you get sucked into drama easily? If you get sucked into other people's drama, you're rewarding their behavior and training them to create more of it through Pavlovian conditioning. You responded to it last time, so surely you'll do so again. What if they double the drama dose—will you respond even quicker?

If you find yourself getting sucked into drama repeatedly, it may be because drama is filling a need for you. Or perhaps you fear the consequences of not buying into it and being left out.

If you want to help someone rise out of their dramatic story, then respond with kindness, but without rewarding the dramatic behavior or judging it. You might even have the courage to show (not tell) that there are better ways to get your attention.

Humans are complex, and it takes a certain level of awareness to not feed off drama. You always have a choice in how you want to respond to any behavior. Instead of taking it personally and firing back, give it some distance and try to understand why the other person is writing a storyline based on drama. When you respond with courage and love instead of fear, you might choose to pour water on the fire instead of fuel. In doing so, you will naturally help elevate the other person out of their own drama, instead of magnifying it by adding your own story.

So next time you find yourself in a situation where someone is calling for drama, watch your response. Do you have the courage not to get sucked into it and let it pass like a quick storm on a warm summer's night?

Create your relationships without drama by facing challenges with courage instead of fear, by being conscious about not defaulting into stories that don't serve you and your relationships. When you do that, there is no story dividing you and them. Instead, there is more understanding. More growth. More play. More depth. More truth.

You can also use what I call "turtle wisdom"—pull your head in and let the shower go past.

THE POOP SHOWER

It's time to introduce you to what I call "poop showers." When someone is operating from a place of fear, the story they're holding on to can get out of control and turn into a poop shower. These are no fun! Let me give you a few examples.

You come home from an extra-long day at work, and your partner is grumpy and yells at you for no apparent reason. You are confused as to what you did wrong. You are doing your best to provide for your family. Why are they not acknowledging how hard you are working?

Your partner might hold on to a story from their childhood when their mom or dad wasn't around much, and they equate not being around to not being loved. Instead of addressing the emotions, your partner showers you with an outburst, fueled by the fear of abandonment.

Or maybe your father is screaming at you when you tell him about your upcoming adventure to Patagonia. You wonder why he can't be happy for you. His screaming might be powered by fear because he is worried that something might happen to you.

How do you respond to those situations? If you tap into your courage, you will be able to respond with compassion. But tap into fear, and you will most likely fight back. Two poop showers turning into an ugly waterfall! Sometimes putting distance between you and the challenging episode gives you time and space to collect your thoughts and not be so reactive. It allows you to respond with compassion, love, and kindness.

When I told my mom about my motorcycle adventure along the Silk Road, she was upset. Even though I've been on many adventures ever since my late teens, this one seemed to top them all. We had a few discussions that were difficult, and it was clear to me that she was reacting from a place of fear.

I received a major poop shower when my mom made a few unintentionally hurtful comments about my dad, my brother, and me that had nothing to do with the upcoming adventure. It wasn't malicious (my mom is one of the kindest humans I know). Her behavior was rooted in fear.

With tears in my eyes, I reminded myself not to take her remarks personally, and to respond with understanding and kindness. I went to my room and sat in silence for a few minutes to wash away her comments and to not move into fear-based reactions. For a moment I felt like the worst daughter in the world. I remembered to come from love and courage in response to her fear. I knew she was trying her best. We all are.

To be honest, I wasn't aware of the level of fear she carried until I got a message during the trip that was very sobering. "I am glad that you are OK and enjoying the adventure because I couldn't bear to lose you." She was scared that her only daughter wouldn't come back from a trip like this. When I saw that message, it hit me hard, and I felt bad for not having had the awareness of her pain. I felt selfish. Despite the obvious dangers, it never crossed my mind that I wouldn't come back.

You can't live your life based on your parents' stories. You must write our own, and it takes courage to do so.

I made sure to include my mom by sharing stories (sometimes a little censored so as not to worry her!) and images from the journey. At one point she said, "I wish I was on this trip with you!"

Upon my safe return I told her that this was one of the deepest and most incredible journeys I've ever been on and she responded with a knowing smile, "You say that about every adventure." True. I cannot wait for the next one.

Make sure that when you do get a poop shower, you don't adopt that experience as a disempowering story. Remember, you are the author of your own stories and you have the power to transform them.

THE TRANSFORMATION CYCLE

Why are stories so impactful when it comes to living boldly? Because a repetitive thought or story can turn into a belief. Your beliefs influence your actions. Your actions shape your habits. And your habits determine your results. This is why it is so important to pay attention to your stories: they create your beliefs, habits, and results.

You are the creator of your own stories. Your mind is infinitely powerful, and you can choose to adopt almost any story and belief you want to!

The transformation cycle is a process that will help you uncover the stories holding you back so that you can adopt a belief system that supports you on your journey to courage. It takes time and effort to shape your belief system, but it's definitely worth it.

Let's walk through the three steps to transforming your stories.

1. OBSERVE YOUR THOUGHTS

Awareness is the first step in transforming your stories, beliefs, and habits.

Be the observer. Observe your thoughts, stories, and beliefs. Just watch what's going through your mind. As you pay attention to your thoughts, you will notice certain patterns. For example, you might realize that every time you get an opportunity to step up professionally, you play small to stay safe.

You may find that you are being more critical of yourself than your worst enemy, or that every time you have a chance to step up and take a risk, you back down because you fear failure. Or, perhaps you're doubting your work, even though you are incredibly talented. Be aware of what comes up. Don't judge; just observe.

I'm not saying it's as easy as telling yourself that your frog will turn into a prince if you kiss him. It's about being aware of your stories, and then deciding whether you want to change them consciously.

Also, be aware of any new stories you are writing. What meaning are you giving to an experience? Life is full of events, and at each turn, you can choose your story. Which one will you choose?

2. REWRITE YOUR STORIES

Once you've become aware of the stories you tell yourself, it's time to rewrite some and feed your mind with stories that support you in becoming more courageous.

But first, let's make sure you absolutely have the motivation to rewrite some of your stories. Ask yourself, "Do I really want to change this story, or is it just giving me comfort or fulfilling a certain need?" Often times, your stories may be meeting a certain need, even while holding you back from living boldly.

If you are not 100 percent certain that you want to release a story, the chances of you being able to rewrite it are very slim. If some of your stories are fulfilling a core need, such as the need to be loved, it will be tougher to change them. Find another way to feel loved so you can leave the old story behind. For example, if one of your stories is around fulfilling your need for love and attention through causing drama (because that is how you used to get attention from a parent), can you think of more rewarding ways to fulfill this need?

At the beginning of each year, I grab my journal and write down all the beliefs I would like to adopt or let go of.

Some of my recent beliefs I jotted down are:

- I keep my heart open, no matter what.
- People generally have good intentions.
- I'm an alchemist and can turn any situation into a positive one.
- I'm adaptable and able to gracefully surrender to whatever challenge comes my way.
- I trust that the universe always has my back.

So instead of blaming your parents for making mistakes, adopt the empowering belief that "they did the best they could with what they had." You can choose to rewrite the stories that have been controlling your life.

Some experiences might have been incredibly difficult, leaving behind deep wounds and scars. Be gentle and patient with yourself. Take one step at a time and seek help from a therapist or close friend when you need it.

I sometimes repeat my beliefs in my mind at the beginning of a meditation. You could also write them on notecards and read them before going to bed. Find a way to remind yourself of your new beliefs, whether that's repeating them in your mind, sleeping on your notecards, or posting them on your mirror. Whatever feels right for you is perfect.

Keep an eye on the stories you choose to let go of, because they may creep back up every now and then to test you.

3. TAKE CONSISTENT ACTION

Once you have clarity on the stories and beliefs you want to adopt, you need to consistently feed them by following through with action. You can't just visualize your beliefs and hope that magic will happen all on its own. You actually have to take action. A lot of action!

For example, if you want to believe that you have the courage to make a big impact in this world, find a way to make a small impact in someone's life right now. Make it a habit to create ripple effects by leaving love notes for your loved ones, making someone a cup of tea, helping a co-worker with a task without being asked, sending someone flowers, or picking up trash.

The consistency and repetition of your actions will help you form new beliefs that will shape your habits. Your new habits, based on empowering stories and beliefs, will enable you to tap into your courage every single day. And those new habits will lead you to the results you desire.

TRAVEL TUNES

Try on some of these empowering beliefs or create some of your own.

- I am the author of my own stories.
- My thoughts and beliefs are supporting me.
- I am living boldly and without regrets.

PIT STOP: SHAPING YOUR BELIEFS

It's time to start actively shaping your belief systems.

Write down all the new beliefs you want to adopt. Your beliefs can be about you, or about the world around you. To get you started, let me give you a few examples of empowering beliefs:

- I have the courage to make a big impact in this world.
- People fundamentally want to see me succeed and conspire for my success.
- I am the author of my own stories.
- My beliefs are supporting me in living boldly.
- I am abundant and attract an abundance of opportunities.
- My friends are amazing humans and we've always got each other's backs.
- I always respond with kindness.

Rewrite your stories and beliefs and watch as your actions, habits, and results shift along with them.

TRAVEL JOURNAL

Here are a few more questions for you to ponder on your journey to courage:

- How are your stories impacting you? Are they helping you to live boldly? Or are they holding you back?
- What stories are you telling yourself that are holding you back from living boldly?
- Observe your thoughts, beliefs, and behaviors over the next few weeks and write down all the stories that are not serving you.
- Ask some of your closest friends if they have noticed anything you could change to become a better person.

STORIES ARE HISTORY
HISTORY OF PAST EXPERIENCES
SUM OF PAST EXPERIENCES = US!

CHANGE STORIES = CHANGE IDENTITY

PRINCIPLE 2: TRUTH

When you know and honor your own truth, you don't have to live according to others' expectations. You feel in alignment with yourself, which gives you the ability to live more boldly. You are not afraid to step up and stand out. You feel safe, knowing that you are congruent with yourself and loved for who you are, flaws and all!

At the same time, when you stand in your truth you will also have the courage to respect and honor anyone else's truth without judgment, no matter how different you are.

WHAT'S YOUR TRUTH?

Understanding and honoring your truth helps you to tap into courage because your decisions and actions are not cluttered with outside noise or stories that don't serve you.

How do you find and embrace your truth? Let's begin by determining what's important for you in your life—your core values.

Your values are what make your heart happy. They are the internal codes that guide you to behave in a certain way that rings true for you. When you understand your values and act in accordance with them, you honor yourself and feel at peace with who you are and where you are headed. This comes with a certain level of liberation and ultimately allows you to step into courage, even despite fear. If you are feeling "off" or unfulfilled in your life, your career, or your relationship choices, it's likely you're not living according to your values. You might not consciously realize that this is happening.

KNOW YOUR GUIDING PRINCIPLES

"It's not hard to make decisions when you know what your values are."
—Roy Disney

When you embrace your values, making the difficult and brave decisions becomes a lot easier. Let me give you some examples. One of my highest values is freedom. In order to stay true to myself, I generally choose to avoid any agreements that make me feel like my wings are being clipped. I need to feel a sense of freedom in whatever I do, or I might feel a little unfulfilled and out of alignment with myself.

Love and trust are two other values that are incredibly important for me. If I don't trust myself and the people closest to me, and if I am not able to give and receive an abundance of love, then I am not living according to my truth and I need to change something in order to feel aligned again.

Getting your values straight will bring you the confidence to make bold decisions without feeling torn or betraying yourself and your integrity. You will be able to stand up for what you believe is right with conviction, courage, and kindness, and your actions wills inspire others to do the same.

Knowing your truth is also about understanding who you are—not what you do or what you own, but who you are as a human being. Your titles, certificates, and possessions are not who you are. They may support you in living how you want to live, but they don't define you.

Your truth is defined and owned by you and you alone. It's your internal software. That's why there is no point in trying to change someone to suit your needs. Your loved ones have their own truth. Just like an elastic band, if you stretch it in a different direction, it will always bounce back.

STAND IN YOUR TRUTH

Once you know your truth, courageously honor and stand up for it—even when it feels easier not to.

When you own your truth, living courageously becomes almost natural because you come from a place of integrity, a place that feels like home. Your decisions will become clearer and more purposeful because they'll be aligned with your core values. Instead of being influenced by fear, your actions will be determined by the guiding principles you choose to live by.

Having clear values gives you the courage to maintain your integrity in situations or relationships that pressure you to act according to other people's values, intentionally or not.

ARE YOU OWNING YOUR TRUTH?

How do you know if you are owning your truth?
You know you are living in your truth when . . .

- You feel free from others' expectations.
- You don't sacrifice your values in order to manipulate an outcome.
- You feel balanced and aligned with yourself.
- You respect others for who they are, and you don't try to change them in order to suit your own needs.
- You don't need or seek outside validation.
- You feel a calm certainty that you are on the right path.
- You are not scared to share your thoughts, even though you risk not being accepted by some people.
- You don't define yourself by what you own or what you do, but by who you are.
- You feel content and at peace most of the time, no matter the circumstances.
- You don't compromise your truth for fear of not being loved or of not being good enough.
- You stand up and speak up for what's right.

It takes courage to be unapologetically you—the best version of you! Truth supports you in living your best version boldly.

RESPECT FOR YOURSELF AND OTHERS

When you stand by your truth, you will have the courage to respect yourself. You'll also have the ability to respect, value, and acknowledge others, even if their values are completely different than yours. In other words, you can disagree with someone without disrespecting them.

Respect, both for yourself and for others, is about acceptance without judgment, embracing your flaws and accepting theirs, standing in your truth, and allowing them to do the same.

The major obstacle standing between you and respect for yourself and others is fear. A fear of not being loved, a fear of being judged, a fear of not being good enough, a fear of not being worthy, a fear of not belonging.

For example, if you have a fear of not being loved, it might seem easier to compromise your values and act according to someone else's desires in order to be loved. However, letting someone dictate your truth is neither sustainable nor fulfilling. Sooner or later, you will feel resentful. Or, you may find yourself in a situation where you are stuck in a truth that is not yours, leaving you feeling lost. Remember: when you honor your truth, you will be loved for who you are, by people who also courageously stand in their truth.

If you don't respect yourself and your truth, you are undermining your own courage. If you don't respect your truth, it is likely others won't, either!

One of my friends recently joined the dating game and has seen an interesting evolution of the men she was attracting, thanks to stepping back into her truth. In the beginning, she was struggling to stay in her truth because of past experiences that taught her a fear of not being worthy. Her fear unconsciously led her to respond to messages in a way that was inauthentic to her in order to "be liked." Moving away from her truth not only took her out of alignment, but it also attracted guys to a *perception* of her, rather than her true, wonderful self.

She started working on owning and respecting her truth again, rather than compromising her values, desires, and beliefs for the sake of being "liked." That subtle shift changed the types of guys she was attracting. She began to attract men who were not only a match for her, but who also displayed the same level of realness and respect for themselves and others. By stepping back into her own truth, she found the types of people who love her for who she is.

A person who unshakingly and wildly owns their truth is incredibly attractive. Imagine someone who is passionate, stands up for their beliefs, and feels comfortable in their skin because they know there is nothing to hide; they are living authentically. This person exudes charisma and draws you in, even if you don't agree with their views. Living your truth is extremely powerful.

Now imagine someone who doesn't live by their values and isn't consistent with their actions. That person may be perceived as inauthentic, or you may feel like something is slightly off when you interact with them. You will find it hard to fully trust them.

Respect yourself and own your truth, and you will attract people into your life who do the same—people who want to play in your playground without changing you. When you respect your own truth and stay true to your values, you will be surrounded by people who love and respect the real you, not just an image or perception of you.

BUT I REALLY DON'T LIKE YOUR OPINIONS!

What if you really don't agree with someone's viewpoints? Or what if someone is not respecting your truth? Are you still able to respect theirs?

Respect does not mean agreeing with everything and everyone. In fact, when you stand in your truth, you most likely won't be able to do that.

In any given situation, you can choose to behave from a lower, fear-driven level—which includes disrespect—or, you can take the high road and respond with respect. Respect is about treating someone with dignity even if you disagree. Respect comes from love and invites courage. Disrespect comes from fear.

This is where your courage boundaries will be tested. You know you are gracefully owning your truth and respecting others when you can disagree with someone—or even feel appalled by their opinions—yet have the ability to show respect and acknowledge their journey. You don't need to be disrespectful or rude. It is so much more fruitful to have a debate without personal attacks.

During my studies I had the opportunity to do an economic research project with the Swiss embassy in South Africa. While playing squash at a local gym near my house in Pretoria, I met a handsome young man who asked me out for dinner. The dinner was great, but my date took me by surprise, and not in a good way! He made a few racist comments that rattled me. I'm not easily shocked, but here I was sharing dinner with an intelligent, fun, kind man who, as a result of his upbringing, had adopted some incredibly racist views.

If there's one thing that gets under my skin more than anything, it's racism. In the face of racism, it takes me quite a bit of effort and a reminder that "I own my truth and respect others" to stay gracious. My low-level response would have been to close down, judge, disrespect, and walk out on him—but that would not have gotten either of us anywhere. Instead, I tried my hardest to stay open and understand his views, and what ensued was a great discussion about the origin of his opinions. I learned something new (and politely declined a second date).

I recently was tested on this principle again. We had just crossed the border into Kazakhstan, our last stop along the Silk Road, when my bike, King Giorgio, got yet another flat tire. Stranded on the side of the road, a Russian biker and his girlfriend stopped and came to the rescue. Vladimir was unbelievably helpful, and we agreed to drink vodka together in Almaty later that night. As Vladimir and Svetlana walked into the bar, he greeted us with "Heil Hitler." I was sure I must have misheard. I realized I hadn't misunderstood when he proudly showed off his swastika chest tattoo and announced that he was a Nazi. For the first time in a long time, I was speechless. After catching my breath, rather than moving into anger, disgust, or judgment (I didn't completely succeed, as I was totally judging by then), I reminded myself to stay curious and not disrespect him. Vlad shared how he grew up with both a Nazi and communist grandparent, and it became clear where his racist beliefs came from.

This encounter was such a great example of how quickly you can shift your perception of someone. Here I was, stranded on the side of the road with a fellow biker helping me, thinking how kind he was. A few hours later, I heard all about his racist views and was judging him for it.

Owning your truth gives you the courage to show respect, even when faced with people, situations, or viewpoints you can't connect with or even comprehend. You can show dignity and respect toward others, but also choose to bow out of spending time together.

If you come from a place of fear, you will be more prone to act based on your judgments or conclusions, missing out on the evolution and lessons you can gain from different perspectives.

Even in the face of disrespect, you can always choose to respond with kindness and respect. Lead the way and others will follow.

I'm convinced that we would have more evolved societies if we managed to respond and engage on a higher level by treating each other with respect, instead of instantly reacting to every judgment or opinion. We'd live together more harmoniously, respecting each other's beliefs without trying to force anyone to conform to our own belief systems. Everyone benefits when you stay open-minded and try to understand others instead of staying stuck in judgment. *Namaste!*

DON'T *NAMASTE* ME!

I used to sit in yoga classes finding it hard to whisper *namaste* at the end because I felt like a phony, and also because I just wanted to keep lying flat on the floor in the final rest pose of Shavasana. I'm not some Indian guru; I'm a privileged white girl wearing activewear, so why do I need to say an expression I hardly comprehend? It wasn't until my motorbike trip through the Himalayas in Nepal that I not only realized how judgmental I had been, but I also discovered the true meaning of *namaste.*

Namaste is the standard greeting in Nepal, and it is incredibly beautiful and so relevant to the principle of truth. When passing others, the Nepalese stop everything and anything they are in the middle of doing, put their hands together, look you in the eyes, and say *namaste.* There is this beautiful moment, a few seconds of undivided attention, connection, and pure presence between humans.

The meaning of *namaste* in Sanskrit roughly translates to, "the spirit within me salutes the spirit in you." Or, to paraphrase, "honor your truth, but also honor everyone else's."

That is exactly what respect is about: honoring someone else's truth without letting go of your own. Respect means loving someone, because at the core we are all the same. OK, I think I'm starting to go too metaphysical on you, so let's talk about missionaries instead (no, I'm not talking about sex—sorry, that's for another book!).

HOW TO RESPECTFULLY DISAGREE

I remember when, as a child, I started to rebel against certain nonsensical behaviors. I've always struggled to understand and accept the approach many missionaries take. I found missionaries often try to force their religious beliefs onto others without honoring or respecting their centuries-old beliefs. Even though I disagree wholeheartedly with this approach, it doesn't give me the right to disrespect missionaries as people. They are merely living and standing up for their own truths, whether I agree with it or not.

It's OK to disagree with someone's opinions, but you can always voice your opinion in a graceful way, without showing disdain or judgment.

This reminds me of a teenager who truly embraced the principle of truth.

I was sitting in front of a kebab shop in a tiny Turkish village on the Black Sea when I met Asil. He was the teenage brother of the guy running the shop. Armed with broken English and Google Translate, Asil inquired about our adventure, culture, and religious beliefs. Knowing that he was a very devoted Muslim, I felt a bit reserved sharing that I am not religious. But I didn't want to lie, so I shared my thoughts openly.

He reacted with love and respect. He acknowledged my different views without stepping out of his own truth. After sharing his beliefs without judging mine, he even invited me to ride the new bicycle that he was so proud of, which I joyfully did.

He touched my heart by acknowledging my different views with respect and without compromising his own values.

TRUTH TRAPS

There are a few traps that might challenge your resolve to honor your truth. Let's look at five behaviors that generally push you away from living your truth. Once you are aware of them, it's a lot easier to avoid them.

ENTITLEMENT

Entitlement can easily pull you out of integrity. It's a behavior some people display that originates from a belief that they deserve certain privileges, often to the detriment of others or their surroundings. And it can come with a level of arrogance, ignorance, and disregard.

A perfect example of this is feeling entitled to trash our environment without a sense of respect for nature. Or feeling deserving of social privileges, to the detriment of others—such as being rude to a waitress because the beer is not cold enough. Or shooting wildlife and posting pictures on social media with the trophy. Or watering the perfect lawn every day in a drought.

Entitlement will never bring you closer to your truth. In fact, entitlement may be a reaction to a fear of not being good enough or a fear of not being "seen."

IGNORANCE

Ignorance is entitlement's best friend! The two support and enhance each other. Ignorance means a lack of knowledge or awareness. It's turning a blind eye to issues. For example, walking into a Buddhist temple with shoes on due to of a lack of cultural awareness is ignorance. So is believing that the world is flat because you reject science, or denying that global warming is happening, or believing everything authorities preach without questioning it.

To avoid ignorance and become more conscious, seek to understand. Ask more questions. Turn a lack of understanding into an opportunity to learn and grow. The more you open your mind, the more you will evolve into the best version of yourself without falling into fear-based ignorance.

When you own your truth with courage, you will be more likely to consider opposing viewpoints without getting stuck in judgment or disrespect.

Ignorance is not always bliss.

MAKING ASSUMPTIONS

Don't make assumptions! A fear of being disliked or not being loved can lead you to interpret someone else's actions as if they mean something about you. Choosing not to make it about you allows you to stay in your truth and respect their truth instead of feeling insecure or fearful.

For example, if your partner tells you that he needs space, you could choose to believe that means he doesn't love you, or that he's rejecting you. Most likely, it just means that he needs more space! By listening, paying attention, and honoring his truth and yours, you'll be able to overcome your initial assumptions.

Imagine your best friend is going through a challenging time and doesn't feel like catching up right now, because this is how he deals with pain. Does that mean that he doesn't want to be your friend anymore? Highly unlikely. But because you might have a different way of going through a challenge, you may draw false conclusions. Don't make assumptions. And don't make it about you.

If you come from a place of fear, you might have a tendency to take things personally. With courage, you can respect and acknowledge someone's needs even if you don't understand them. Remember, you are not in control of anyone else's truth.

LACK OF APPRECIATION

A lack of appreciation for places, people, and moments seems more common now than ever.

People are throwing moments and things away like it's their job! There is a constant striving for more, more, and yet more . . . only to realize that more (of anything) often doesn't bring you closer to your truth or make you happier. It's so easy to get lost in this cycle.

Remember to stop and smell the flowers every now and then. Gratitude and appreciation help you to remember your truth, which is usually not found in more stuff. A daily practice of gratitude is like a pit stop that refuels your soul and helps you focus on what's truly important. This simple practice brings you closer to your truth and allows you to step into your courage.

INCONSISTENCY

Not knowing and not owning your truth often results in inconsistency, and that leads to insecurities, fears, and doubts. Inconsistency is not very attractive!

Staying consistent in your thoughts, decisions, and actions will help you build a strong foundation for truth. If you waver, you are shaking your foundation and you'll begin to doubt yourself. And doubt invites fears.

Commit to your truth and do so consistently. Courage loves consistency.

Own your truth and expect to be loved for who you are, not what you do or what you own. Some people might choose to leave your playground and that's OK, because they are not the ones that will help you become the best version of yourself.

If you stay true to yourself, you'll be loved for who you truly are.

TRAVEL TUNES

It's time to turn up the music! Here are some travel tunes for you to put on repeat.

- I own my truth with consistency.
- I will always be loved for who I am.
- I honor and respect others as they are.

PIT STOP: DEFINING YOUR VALUES

Redefine your values. Ask yourself the following questions:

- What is important for me in my life?
- What makes me happy?
- What fulfills me?

Write down any words that come up, then narrow them down to three-to-five values that are non-negotiable for you. Some examples of values may include: courage, truth, respect, fun, friendship, love, gratitude, growth, generosity, passion, peace, wealth, vitality, wisdom, and curiosity.

Take some time to jot down anything that comes to mind when you think about your life and what truly fulfills you. Once you know what makes your heart happy, you can be more conscious about honoring your truth.

TRAVEL JOURNAL

Grab your Courage Map and write down your thoughts on the following questions:

- What are your values? What makes you happy?
- What do you stand for?
- What do you stand against?
- Is there anywhere in your life you feel like you are compromising your truth?

- What is one thing you can do right now to boldly step into your truth?
- When do you find it hard to respect someone else's truth?
- How can you be more respectful of others?

PRINCIPLE 3: INTENTIONS

Everything starts with an intention, whether you jump out of bed with a big smile, buy someone a thoughtful gift, or decide to live courageously. It all starts with intention.

"Intention is the mother of all change."
—Abhijit Naskar

Intentions are thoughts that guide your actions and support you on your journey to living boldly. Intentions are thoughts with direction. The desire to live more courageously starts with an intention followed by action. Be intentional about living boldly—you get to choose your adventure.

CHOOSE YOUR JOURNEY

Think of life as a road trip. Your vision is your ultimate destination, the place you are traveling toward. Your values are the compass showing you which turns to take at a crossroad. Your intentions are your style of traveling and they determine whether you hop, skip, run, climb, ride, drive, skate, or swim. Your actions are the path you choose.

Use your values to make sure you are making decisions that are aligned with your truth. Remember: the values you worked on in the previous principle are here to support you in taking the "right" actions in line with your truth. When you are at a crossroads on your journey, they will help you decide whether to turn right or left.

Next, choose your vehicle or style of traveling: your intentions. Your intentions are derived from your values. If they don't support your values, you will feel out of alignment. It's like hiking Mount Everest in a bikini or surfing in your snowboard gear.

Your intentions determine how you want to show up in the world. You might choose to show up with kindness, or curiosity, or courage. Or all of the above.

Let's see how this all fits together. I shared with you earlier that one of my highest values is love—not just romantic love, but the unconditional kind of love for all beings. Based on that core value, one of my intentions is "to live with an open heart." This is something I have to keep reminding myself of when I'm experiencing something that makes me want to close my heart.]]]Another intention that supports my value of trust is "to surrender and know that everything always works out exactly how it is meant to."

You choose how you want to show up for yourself and others.

HOW DO YOU WANT TO SHOW UP?

Setting intentions is essentially directing your energy and choosing how you want to show up in life.

Your intentions inspire your actions. Since you are reading this book, one of your intentions is most likely to live boldly. This intention is leading you to take actions, such as designing your Courage Map and applying the principles in this book.

At the beginning of every year, I get clear on how I want to show up in the world by writing down my intentions. These may include "I courageously keep my heart open," or "I always respond with kindness," or "I move through life gracefully," or "I use my resources to make an impact."

Take some time to write down your intentions by asking yourself: How do I want to show up in the world? Then, keep this in mind when you take action toward your vision. Remind yourself of your intentions when you feel pulled off path. Course-correct and come back to them, so that you feel in alignment with your truth and are able to move boldly.

Intentions are basically your style of traveling. They are incredibly powerful. When you don't know where to put your energy, you may feel scattered, confused, or incongruent with yourself. Intentions help you funnel your energies. They set the tone and influence your thoughts, actions, and results.

Your intentions also have the power to impact those around you on a very subtle level. For example, the effects of the intention, "I always keep my heart open," have been profound for me. It's not always easy! Whenever I feel my heart close, I keep reminding myself to have the courage to keep it open—even though it might get hurt. Thanks to this intention, my adventures have been even richer, my moments more impactful, and my relationships deeper.

I remember when Mike and I rode into Georgia, crossing the border from Turkey at night. It was raining, and we were drenched, tired, and hungry. When we arrived at the apartment we had booked online, there was no one there to let us in. I felt my grumpiness levels rise—not something that happens very often. With a growling stomach, I walked into a tiny supermarket across the road to buy a snack while we figured out where to sleep.

Even though one of my intentions is to "always keep an open heart," I was not feeling very loving that night. I knew my energy was different and I didn't feel like talking to anyone. It was interesting to observe how the energy of the supermarket lady matched mine. I tried to get the lady's attention with the best smile my grumpy mood could muster but she was busy typing on her phone and couldn't have cared less about me being in her store. I normally feel supported and welcomed in most situations. But this time, because I didn't show up with love in my own heart, I wasn't met with it either, so I walked back out into the rain empty-handed. I'm forever grateful for room service (Mike and I gave up on the apartment and checked into a fancy hotel instead).

It's up to you to shift your energy in order to shift the energy around you. Armed with this awareness, you can intentionally put your energy behind your thoughts and actions again.

I sometimes hear people say things like, "she stole my vibe," or "he took me out of my flow." Nobody can steal your vibe! You choose your vibe. Life may not always be a walk in the park, but trust your ability to be intentional about showing up the way you want to.

CHOOSE YOUR INTENTIONS

It's time to set your intentions. But first, let's look at the difference between goals and intentions. They can appear to be very similar.

The biggest difference is that intentions are not something that you tick off as "done," in the way goals are. Intentions are a way of living. Intentions influence the mode of transport you choose and which music you are going to listen to on your adventures. They support you in achieving your goals and allow you to enjoy the ride in your own style.

And just like you can change your music, you can also adapt and evolve your intentions to suit your purpose. Intentions are fluid, which means you can change and adjust them often. Intentions are not linear, like goals with specific outcomes expected. When you set the intention to "always keep an open heart," you know there will be positive outcomes, but you don't know exactly how or when they will happen.

For example, you might set a goal to launch a new business by the end of the year. Some supporting intentions could be to stay open-minded, to focus on learning, and to stay flexible and adaptable along the way.

Or, you might set a goal to create the deepest and most fulfilling relationship with your partner with the intentions of gracefully going with the flow, staying in your truth, always sharing from the heart, and loving unconditionally.

Set an intention, show up, and then observe what happens—without judgment or attachment.

Let's choose your intentions—intentions that support you in living boldly!

1. PICK YOUR STYLE

First, choose your intentions by asking yourself: "How do I want to show up? What is my style? How do I want to travel toward my goals?"

Your intentions are like the theme for your party. You want to frame them in a positive way—for example, "I choose to be courageous," rather than "I attempt to be less fearful," or "I am kind," instead of "I don't want to be inconsiderate." Intentions fueled by courage are more powerful and sustainable than those fueled by fear.

Take a few minutes to write down who you want to be and how you want to show up. Don't forget to include "I choose to live boldly."

2. PUSH YOURSELF, JUST A LITTLE BIT

You are reading this book because you know that you can and want to be more courageous. You have what it takes to step it up and live a bold life.

When you set your intentions, push yourself a little bit. You will know you are staying too safe by the lack of butterflies in your stomach. You want to feel a sense of excitement when you set your intentions, a sense of infinite possibilities.

Of course, you also want your intentions to be realistic enough for you to be able to live them.

You'd better believe that you can! If you believe, then you will be able to achieve. If you don't, then rewrite your story around that belief (go back to the first principle in this book) and work on yourself until you do. Then commit to yourself by embracing your style wholeheartedly!

As you get more comfortable with your intentions, remember it's OK to adjust your style and adopt different intentions.

3. ALIGN WITH YOUR VALUES

Your intentions must be in line with your values and support you in attaining your vision. Your values, vision, and intentions all play together, just like a beautiful piece of art where different elements come together to create a dazzling picture.

For example, if one of your values is truth, then the intention "I honor my truth and am honest with myself and others" will serve you. On the other hand, an intention like "I protect myself and others by hiding the truth" is not in line with one of your values and will restrict you from living truthfully and boldly.

Go back to the values you've written down and set your intentions in support of them.

4. MANAGE YOUR STATE

Lastly and most importantly, make sure your intentions come from courage instead of fear.

A cluttered and fearful mind will leave you in a state of uncertainty, and your intentions will reflect that. So, before you set your intentions, do whatever it takes to get yourself into a peaceful state of mind, whether that is through meditation, lighting a candle, listening to your favorite music, taking a walk in nature, or drinking a glass of wine or tequila.

Trust what's coming up for you when your mind is relaxed. Your intentions need to come from you, and not be directed or influenced by a partner, a guru, or anyone else. You choose your style.

SET YOUR SAILS

Once you have clarity on your intentions, it's time to set your sails. It will all be smooth sailing until the wind blows from a different side. Then you might have to adjust your sails and course correct. This is where it gets interesting. How do you react when the wind starts blowing you in a different direction? An intention such as "I am adaptable and surrender to the flow of life" might support you here.

On our motorbike journey along the Silk Road, we generally had an idea of where we were heading. But many days, the wind was blowing in a different direction due to unforeseen circumstances. I remember riding through Armenia to the border of Iran to fulfill one of my biggest dreams, to ride my motorbike through Iran, when an unexpected situation changed the course of my journey.

For me, the best kinds of intentions are the ones that come from deep in my heart but have a lightness to them so that, when things don't go as planned, I don't get attached. Instead, I try to see perfection in the imperfection.

UNCONDITIONAL-NESS, THE MOTHER OF ALL INTENTIONS

For the last decade or so I have been really curious about the concept of "unconditional-ness," and one of my intentions is to be more unconditional in all areas of my life. Love is the most obvious one. But there is also unconditional generosity, unconditional kindness, and unconditional understanding.

Unconditional-ness is about having the courage to not make your choices and behavior dependent on external circumstances. Unconditional-ness does not carry any "ifs," such as "if you love me, I will love you too" or "if it's easy, I will be courageous" or "if you do this, I do that." It comes back to standing and acting from your truth, independent of someone else's behavior.

Unconditional-ness means that you (strive to) act in line with your intentions and behave according to your truth, independent of anyone else's actions and behaviors. You choose to love, even when you're not loved back. You are kind even when met with rudeness. You give without expecting to receive. You strive to leave people and places better off.

If I can say on my deathbed that I mastered unconditional-ness in most areas of my life, I will die a very happy woman. The answer to the question, "Would I be happy with my life if I died right now?" should be a resounding yes!

Apply unconditional-ness to being courageous. Don't be courageous only when all the stars align. Choose to be courageous even when it's easier not to.

I'd love to invite you to join me on the quest to unconditional-ness. It is a journey worth embarking on, a journey that helps you not only bring out the best in yourself, but also in those you interact with. Being unconditional leaves people better off. It's a subtle invitation for them to step up too, consciously or unconsciously.

On this quest, observe your intentions behind your words and actions. Be curious and conscious without judging yourself. Are you coming from a place of unconditional-ness or are you projecting your own expectations onto others?

Be intentional about being unconditional. Be intentional about showing up, speaking the truth, and doing the right thing. This will give you the fuel to be courageous despite the fears.

The more you intentionally choose to be courageous, the more you will find that you are acting from a place of truth. There is a huge sense of freedom and liberation that comes with that.

Choose to live boldly.

TRAVEL TUNES

- I choose to be courageous.
- I am unconditional.
- I show up for myself and for others.

PIT STOP: SETTING INTENTIONS

Ready to create your life's perfect vision and set intentions to get you there?

Let's start with your destination. Be intentional about where you are heading by asking yourself the following questions: What is my vision in life? What would I like to be remembered for? What legacy do I want to leave?

Maybe you want to be remembered as someone who dared to

live courageously? Or to leave people better off? Or to be an amazing friend, parent, partner, sister, or daughter? Or to make an impact through entrepreneurship? Or all of that.

If you want to take it a step further, write your own eulogy. What do you want to be remembered for?

Once you have clarity on your vision and values, write down your intentions. How do you want to show up to fulfill your vision? Write down at least five intentions.

TRAVEL JOURNAL

It's time to ponder the following questions. You might want to create a peaceful atmosphere, conducive to setting intentions and adding to your Courage Map; play your favorite music, light a candle, or pour a glass of your favorite drink.

- Where can you be more intentional about being courageous? What needs to happen for you to choose to be courageous?
- Where are you currently not choosing to be courageous?
- How can you be more unconditional? Where or with whom in your life are you being conditional?

PRINCIPLE 4: TRUST

Trust is one of the biggest key drivers to living boldly. Without trust, your actions and decisions are more likely to be guided by uncertainties and fears. Trust supports you in stepping into courage even when you are faced with challenges.

When it comes to living boldly, we are looking at three types of trust: trust in yourself, trust in others, and trust in the process, or "universe" as I like to call it. "I trust that the universe has my back" is one of my biggest beliefs. It allows me to face challenges with courage instead of fear.

I remember when we were walking home in Tbilisi (the capital of Georgia in Central Asia) after a night spent discussing politics with an Iranian refugee at a quiet Iranian bar. Mike asked me, "What do you think would happen if people trusted others more than they trust themselves?"

A brilliant question, as always! "Can I think about this and discuss it with you in the morning?" I replied, sleepy-eyed. I needed some time to ponder and didn't want to rush my answer.

If people trusted others more than themselves, there would be more uncertainty, imbalance, and less authenticity in the human experience. Instead of standing in your own truth and making decisions based on that, you would be swaying from your core. When you have clarity on your truth, you will have the courage to trust yourself, your decisions, and actions. If you don't have that trust, you will find it harder to make quick decisions, and you'll instead second-guess everything and slip into fear-driven behaviors.

There is so much advice out there. Everyone is an expert of some sort and wants to give you their well-meaning advice. Not all of that advice is equally beneficial, or even in alignment with where you are headed. How do you navigate through a labyrinth of advice? How do you know which advice to follow? By trusting in yourself. Assume that you already have the answers within yourself, even if they are not apparent in the moment.

Trust in yourself first and foremost. And then trust that the universe always has your back. Sometimes, when you're hit with the most difficult circumstances, that's a really tough thing to believe! However, when you do, you will live so much more boldly. Of course, this does not mean being naive or negligent. Trust is rooted in experience, information, and intuition.

TRUST IN YOUR ABILITIES

When you get clear on your abilities and capabilities in any area of life or business, you will develop the courage to make your own decisions, free from other people's opinions and stories. Knowing and trusting your strengths can help you make courageous decisions, whether that means saying yes or no to something with confidence.

Before starting my around-the-world motorbike journey, I didn't have that much experience riding off-road or in the clogged traffic of massive cities, and my abilities were mediocre at best. However, two weeks of riding motorbikes through Italy with one of my best friends gave me practice that would prove beneficial to my adventure along the Silk Road. It was on that two-week trip through Italy that I earned my "Italian driving license," as Mike jokingly called it when he followed me, zipping through the Turkish traffic in Istanbul—a city notorious for its crazy drivers. I improved my riding skills, which made me more courageous. I wasn't reckless, but I was able to trust my own abilities.

However, my off-roading skills were yet to be developed. So when Mike and I were riding through the Georgian mountains, I usually allowed myself to fall behind, setting my own pace rather than following him at high speed. I had to trust in my own abilities, not his. I learned to take calculated risks by pushing myself without being reckless.

Remember: courage is not recklessness. Courage is about trusting yourself and your abilities and making brave decisions in line with what you can do, not in line with what others are saying or doing.

Learn to trust yourself. The more you do, the more you will come from a place of courage. It may take some practice to fully trust. Set the intention, and then be conscious about following it.

Trust yourself to go after your wildest dreams. Trust in your ability to live boldly.

THE UNIVERSE HAS YOUR BACK

"The universe has your back" is one of my core beliefs that supports me in making brave decisions. I recommend you adopt it too

If you believe that the universe has your back, you will find it easier to step into courage because you know that things always work out exactly how they are meant to, even if it doesn't seem that way in the moment.

Pay attention to the winks the universe gives you. I love a metaphor that one of my friends shared with me: First, the universe throws a feather at you. Then, if you ignore it, next comes a brick. And if you ignore that, you'll get hit by a truck!

For example, you might find that you're catching a cold every few weeks because you're over-committed, overworking, and not looking after yourself. Maybe you have some other unhealthy habits thrown into the mix. But you ignore the signs and keep going on the way you have been. That's the feather.

Then your health starts to take a serious hit and you are in bed for a week. So you pump yourself up with vitamins and get back to work as soon as you feel slightly OK.

A few months pass. Now the truck is in sight, as your health declines even more. Hopefully, you see the truck coming before it hits you, and decide to change a few of your habits . . . maybe you book a vacation to disconnect and rejuvenate, or you say no to a few social commitments in order to rest.

On our journey through the Stans (Azerbaijan, Turkmenistan, Uzbekistan, Tajikistan, Kyrgyzstan, and Kazakhstan) my motorcycle, King Giorgio, started to get a little bit tired—and so did I! We'd been pushing it hard, riding long days on dirt roads. When we reached Tajikistan, a country famous for its mountains, we decided to take a road one travel blogger described as "not for the faint-hearted, for diehard bikers only."

I'm certainly not a diehard biker, but we thought the author of the post must be exaggerating, so we decided to ignore his advice and take that route. It turned out that he was not exaggerating! The road was challenging, with waist-deep river crossings, muddy roads, washboard gravel, and mind-blowing views through ever-changing terrain and snowy mountains. We'd been riding all day and still had a long way to go before reaching our accommodation. After crossing a river that left us wet to our underpants, the road turned into switchback after switchback up into the snow as the sun was setting behind the mountain tops. With frozen hands and feet, I was riding faster than I should have, rushing to get to a hot shower and food. Suddenly my bike slipped on a mud patch. As I accelerated to get out of the mud, I lost control over the bike and rode off the side of a cliff. I somehow managed to jump off the bike mid-flight and tumbled a few meters down the cliff. Meanwhile, King Giorgio was doing somersaults about thirty meters down the face of the mountain.

As I was lying on my back holding my very bruised leg, shaking uncontrollably and tears running down my face, I realized that it was a miracle I got away without any serious injuries (thanks to protective gear!). King Giorgio, on the other hand, looked very broken. In fact, on closer inspection, we thought he might not be rideable again. I got on the back of Mike's bike to ride to the next village. After a three-hour ride in the dark, we arrived just after midnight. Despite the surrealness of the situation, we still managed to laugh as we stopped to look at the countless stars. Here we were with my bike stuck on the side of a cliff on the Afghan border in Tajikistan, under one of the most beautiful starry night skies I had ever seen. You couldn't make this up even if you tried!

The next day we got a truck to pick up King Giorgio. And to my surprise and delight, a very resourceful and crafty Tajik mechanic managed to patch him back together!

This accident was a big brick that hit me right across the face (or shall I say leg). I took the warning sign seriously and from then on slowed down. We also didn't ride crazy roads in the dark anymore. This one brick moment may have saved our lives.

Pay attention to the "messages" and then trust that the universe has your back. Trust enables you to live more boldly.

FOLLOW STRANGERS

"You are a bit naive!" my mom would occasionally tell me when yet again I did something that seemed a little too trusting. And I even believed her sometimes. Occasionally, I've thought that maybe *I am* a bit naïve—until I realized that more often than not, it is trust that may be perceived as naivety. I trust in myself and in my judgment so much that I *do* sometimes follow strangers. And of course, there have also been many times when I didn't because something felt off, rightly or wrongly. My intuition gives me the cues, and I trust them. This has led to some of the richest moments in my life.

It was a cloudy morning when Mike and I rode into a tiny mountain village in Turkey, on our way to what's known as "the most dangerous road in the world." We thought it would be smart to pick up some snacks there, just in case we got stuck on the mountain or needed to camp somewhere along the way. I left Mike with the bikes and strode off toward a little grocery store.

The shop assistant greeted me with a friendly smile. I used my best sign language and pointed at the bread hanging in a brown paper bag from the shelf. An older gentleman wearing neat pants and a checkered shirt walked in, looked at me, said something in Turkish, then waved for me to follow him. So I did.

We walked outside, past Mike, who asked, "What are you doing?" with a puzzled look on his face.

"I'm just following strangers," I said with a smirk. Then I added, "If not back in fifteen minutes, you might want to come and look for me."

Ibrahim led me to a bakery down the road, where he bought me a loaf of bread straight out of the oven. I was so excited. Fresh bread! Oh, how I love gluten! My belly was growling and I took a big bite of warm bread—delicious! We took a few selfies with the bakery lady, who had the kindest eyes, and Ibrahim walked me back to the store.

Ibrahim gestured for me to grab some more groceries. As I handed my wallet to the shop owner—yeah, I usually just gave them my entire wallet so that they could find the right coins and bills (completely trusting that they would do the right thing)—Ibrahim pushed me aside and gave the lady a few bills of Turkish lira. A stranger just bought my groceries! I was speechless! Unconditional generosity is so beautiful.

It was such a perfect moment—an example of what I call "moments of humanity"—and one I will treasure for life: strangers connecting through kindness. An experience based on trusting my intuition to follow a stranger.

Trust in others. But trust in yourself first, so you know *when* to follow strangers. Many of my most magical moments along my adventures happened because I trusted myself and others.

The more you pay attention to your intuition, the more you will be able to trust your judgment, even when the hunch you are getting doesn't make sense at the time.

ASSUME THAT PEOPLE GENERALLY MEAN WELL

This leads me to another one of my core beliefs that you might like to adopt as well: "People generally mean well and do the best they can with what they have." Sometimes the best they can do may not be amazing in your eyes, and that's OK too.

When I recently spoke at a conference in Dallas, Texas, I was being "naive" and left my cash on top of the bench in my hotel room. I forgot to grab it on the way out, and when I came back, it was gone.

At first, I was really disappointed because I trusted in humanity and didn't think that the room attendant would be dishonest. And then I realized that trusting doesn't mean tempting someone unreasonably. Whoever took the cash did the best they could. Trusting is not being silly or tempting faith; trusting is acting in accordance with your intuition and doing so boldly.

One observation that I've made throughout my travels is that when people see you place your trust in them, they automatically want to step up and do their best to live up to your unspoken expectations! It's pretty cool to see. It's as if you lead them by example, showing them that they're trustworthy.

Try it out. You might be pleasantly surprised by an abundance of kindness. You will feel an energy shift from fear and "I don't trust you," to love and "we're all in this together."

When you believe that people mean well, they will often rise up to your belief. Just like when I handed my wallet to a shop assistant to find the right coins. I have not been ripped off once (or maybe I just didn't notice it). It's an assumption that can change the way you live and see the world. On the other hand, if you act as if someone is not trustworthy, they'll probably live up to that expectation too.

On one of our stopovers in a small town in Montenegro, I got up early for a quick swim before hitting the road. It was a steaming hot summer day, so I grabbed a beach towel and walked down the long stairs to the beach barefoot. Halfway down, I discovered a small fruit stall with a middle-aged, grey-haired local farmer selling raspberries. I stopped and told the stall owner that I would come back later to buy some raspberries because I didn't have any money on me.

He didn't speak English, but he seemed to understand. He handed me a basket of freshly picked raspberries and made signs I interpreted as "come back and pay later." I felt a deep sense of appreciation knowing that he trusted me. It made me feel special and I certainly wanted to live up to his expectation. Another moment of humanity: strangers united through courage, kindness, and trust.

THE EYE OF THE HURRICANE

The hurricane metaphor is a great visual that can remind you to trust yourself and help you navigate through storms. Every hurricane has an eye in the center, the area of calm surrounded by the eyewall. It's a ring of the most severe weather and strongest winds.

Use this image of the eye in a hurricane when life sends you a storm, or when there is chaos all around you. Imagine yourself being the calm in the center and try to stay grounded instead of joining the chaos around you. Observe and be aware, but don't allow yourself to be pulled into the storm. From this place of calm, you can make more intelligent and courageous decisions.

Every now and then, when you feel yourself getting dragged into the chaos, remind yourself to stay calm. This metaphor might just help you to move back into your own center so you can respond to your surroundings from a place of trust and courage, rather than reacting from a place of fear.

Next time you find yourself in a fight with your partner, or in a challenging situation in your business, be conscious of the storm. Oftentimes you can't control what's going on around you, nor the fear-based actions and behaviors others may display. But you can always choose to stay calm and trust that the universe has your back. Trust yourself to make the right decisions. Trust yourself to be courageous.

When you fully drop into trust, you will make bolder decisions and take courageous action, because you know that everything is going to work out exactly how it is meant to.

The universe always has your back.

TRAVEL TUNES

- I trust myself.
- The universe always has my back.
- People generally mean well.

PIT STOP: TRUST AND EXPECT THE BEST

For the next thirty days, trust that every person you meet generally means well. In any interaction, whether with a waiter, a friend, a family member, or a colleague, show them that you trust them. If someone gives you a recommendation, rather than questioning it, trust it. If a colleague is offering help, trust that they've got this. Make strangers feel that you trust them and observe what happens.

TRAVEL JOURNAL

Grab your journal and reflect on the following questions:

- What would happen if you trusted your intuition more often? For the next month, make more decisions based on your intuition and see what happens.
- Where in your life do you need to trust more to help you step into courage?
- What bold decision would you make right now if you believed that the universe always has your back?
- Do you remember a time when you trusted your gut instincts? How did you feel?

PRINCIPLE 5: INTUITION

The ability to tap into your intuition allows you to stay true to yourself, take risks, and make courageous decisions, even when those decisions don't seem to make sense to others.

Trusting in your gut also ensures that you are not trapped by what others want you to do or be. Instead, you rely on yourself and your inner wisdom to choose how you live your life courageously.

The late Steve Jobs, co-founder of Apple, said, "Have the courage to follow your heart and intuition. They somehow already know what you truly want to become. Everything else is secondary." He was a great example of someone who trusted his inner wisdom and made massive courageous moves despite a lot of push-back from stakeholders.

Because intuition comes from your unconscious mind, and the unconscious mind processes information much faster than your conscious mind, it allows you to make decisions faster and with certainty. Ultimately, intuition supports you in handling uncertainties with more ease, as you are not relying on outside information. When you tap into your intuition, you don't need to wait until all the ducks are in a row to take a leap.

Intuition supports you in living more effortlessly and courageously because you feel certain despite the presence of fear.

"The only real valuable thing is intuition."
—Albert Einstein

WHAT IS INTUITION?

Intuition is one of the most powerful tools in your toolbox when it comes to living courageously. When you fully trust your inner wisdom, being courageous becomes a habit, a way of living, not a thing you do occasionally.

Intuition is something we are all born with. You know those moments when you get goose bumps out of the blue? Or your hair is standing on your back for no apparent reason? Or 'something' is telling you to remove yourself from a place or situation because it's not quite right, but you don't know why? Or you suddenly feel physical sickness in your stomach?

That's your intuition talking. It's an inner knowledge that is generally spot on! Those seemingly random hunches or signals your unconscious mind gives you are there to guide you in making better decisions.

People often refer to "trusting your intuition" as "following your heart." In fact, many ancient civilizations believed that the heart, not the brain, was the most important part of the body.

So where does intuition come from? Why do we get these unconscious signals? Intuition is based on the subconscious processing of information you have gathered throughout your lifetime of experiences. Your subconscious mind is drawing on past experiences and sending signals through different senses that you sometimes notice with your conscious mind.

Intuition is the bridge between the conscious and unconscious mind, between the logical and the illogical, the analytical and the unsystematic. Intuition can be your most powerful guide if you listen to it.

HELLO INTUITION, ARE YOU THERE?

As mentioned earlier, intuition is something you are born with. However, you may sometimes forget how to tap into it. Experiences and stories clutter your being, moving you away from your core and out of touch with your inner wisdom.

Growing up in Switzerland, intuition was not something people talked about a lot. To be honest, I didn't even fully grasp the concept until I moved to Australia at the age of twenty-three.

Swiss culture is very logical and rational. When I first started reading about intuition and how some of the most impactful people in the world make decisions based on this internal voice, my interest was piqued, and I went on a journey to practice it, rationally! I started to meditate daily, journal more, and pay attention to my emotions and energy levels around people, places, and decisions.

I slowly started to trust my intuition and make decisions based on my "gut feeling" instead of pure logic.

Whenever I need to make a big decision now, or go through shifts in my life or business, I turn to my journal. I go inward first before getting my friends' perspectives. If it's a personal decision, I often don't consult others at all, because I want my decisions to come from my most sincere, purest, unconscious being, from my intuition, my internal guide.

I know my friends want the best for me and always have my back, even when I mess up. Quite often their advice is incredibly valuable and aligns with mine. Sometimes it doesn't. I trust my intuition to guide me and I keep reminding myself to stay courageous as I process my thoughts and ask the tough questions.

When you trust your inner wisdom, others will sometimes perceive you as illogical in your decision-making. Irrational doesn't mean it has to be silly or foolish; it simply means that the decision-making process is not based purely on rational or logical arguments. The knowledge is coming from a different source.

Some of my most courageous and illogical decisions have turned out to be the best ones because they came from trusting my inner wisdom. For example, some of my best hires in business were based purely on intuition, and then I used ration later by reference-checking and doing all that "normal stuff."

When you are living in fear instead of courage, you will be more prone to questioning your intuition or even distrusting it. As a result, you will be more likely to trust everyone else's opinion. The thing is, you don't need a guru; you are your most powerful guru.

SEVEN WAYS TO TAP INTO YOUR INTUITION

1. TUNE IN AND OBSERVE

The more you practice self-awareness, the more you will be able to trust your intuition. It's always communicating with you, but you might not always hear, feel, or see it. The more you connect with yourself and your surroundings, the more you will be able to notice the intuitive hunches. Learn to tune into your body, sensations, thoughts, and feelings. The more you do, the more you will make living courageously a habit, a way of *being*, not doing.

Get really good at observing. Observe yourself, your environment, and other people. Observe how your sensations respond to different situations and people. The more you tune in, the more you will sense the signals and perceive coincidences.

Pay attention to your physical reactions. Do you sometimes feel an increased heartbeat, body pain, or sweaty palms? Also observe your emotions: do you sometimes feel unsettled? This could be your intuition talking.

You don't need to consciously look for signs from the universe, or use the lack of signs as an excuse to not make bold decisions. Trust whatever comes to you, no matter how illogical or irrational.

2. CONNECT WITH YOUR HEART

Your heart is your most powerful organ. It's full of nerve cells that contain knowledge. Listen to it. Put your hand on your heart often to connect with it. What does your heart tell you?

A lot of unconscious information and memories are stored in this organ. There are countless stories of people who, after undergoing a heart transplant, experienced a change in abilities, interests, and preferences based on cellular memories stored in the heart.

Sometimes when I give a keynote address and am intentional about showing up with an open heart and mind, I find myself intuitively sharing insights I didn't even know I had. I don't think I'm channeling aliens. I believe it is because of the experiences, books, and information I have consumed over the years that have all been stored in my subconscious mind or heart. That information becomes accessible when your mind is relaxed and your heart is open.

The more you consciously keep your heart open, the more you will tap into your intuitive being.

3. PRACTICE MINDFULNESS

Mindfulness might be a buzzword at the moment, but there is a reason why. Practicing mindfulness has so many benefits beyond feeling present in the moment. One benefit is perceiving signals from your intuition. This is because practicing mindfulness and meditating regularly helps you cut out the noise that may cloud your intuition.

Sometimes you might be too busy to notice the messages your inner wisdom is sending you. A calm and present mind allows your conscious mind to feel, hear, and see the signals from your unconscious.

If you are new to meditation or have been struggling with it, let go of the outcome. It is completely normal and OK if you do a 10-minute meditation and spend nine of the ten minutes thinking about the world's problems (or your own), what's for dinner, where you will spend your next holiday, a recent conversation you've had, or why your thoughts are drifting off. Make meditation a daily habit and the one minute of pure presence will turn into two and grow from there.

4. EMBRACE SOLITUDE

Consciously find solitude by spending more time alone. This is a great way to learn to reconnect with yourself and tune in to your sensations, thoughts, and emotions.

Embracing solitude might be more challenging for extroverts who love to be surrounded by people and get their energy from others. For introverts, spending time alone comes a lot easier; in fact, it's necessary for us to fill up our batteries.

Take time out every now and then and go out into nature, sit amongst the trees, swim in the ocean, or walk through a park, and do so with complete presence. The more you do, the more you will tune in and become aware of your inner guidance.

And if you struggle to shut down your brain's constant chatter, meditate or feed your brain with a few deeper questions to ponder. The travel journals that follow each principle in this book have a few options to get you started.

5. MAKE DECISIONS FASTER

Remember, intuition helps you to make decisions more quickly because your unconscious mind processes information a lot more rapidly than your conscious mind. So, a great way to practice becoming more intuitive is to force yourself to make decisions faster. When faced with a decision, listen to the first answer that comes up for you and go for it. Practice on smaller decisions first until you become more confident in trusting your intuition, and then use the same intuitive approach for the bigger, more difficult and courageous decisions.

Indecisiveness can make you miss out on a lot of brilliant opportunities and hold you back from making bold decisions. Learn to listen to your internal voice and let your inner guru guide you.

EMPATHY IS HOT

As you learn to tap into your intuition, you will also learn to feel more empathy. Empathy is an evolved human ability to understand and share the feelings of others. It's something that not only makes you a better leader, parent, colleague, or friend in this world, but also something that is very much needed right now.

Developing your intuitive ability will support you in putting yourself in others' shoes without judgment. It helps you to understand someone's feelings so you can respond appropriately. Empathy connects you. It enables you to selflessly share in someone's joy or sadness.

Empathy supports you in courageously doing what's best for the greater good, rather than being self-serving.

When you commit to showing up for yourself and the world with empathy, you will make brave decisions with integrity.

Practice making decisions from your core, rather than asking others to make decisions for you. Your intuition is one of your most impactful tools that can help you live boldly. Learn to tap into it and trust yourself. Sometimes your loved ones might not understand where certain brave decisions are coming from, and that's OK. They may worry and try to keep you safe because they love you. You don't need to be kept safe—you have your intuition to guide you.

Trust yourself to pursue your wildest dreams. Trust in your ability to live boldly.

TRAVEL TUNES

- I trust my hunches.
- My intuition guides me.
- I am capable of empathy.

PIT STOP: TRUSTING YOUR INTUITION

For the next thirty days, fully trust your intuition. Whenever faced with a choice, ask your inner wisdom for an answer and trust whatever comes up first, even if it doesn't make sense in the moment.

TRAVEL JOURNAL

Grab your Courage Map and reflect on the following questions:

- Do you remember a time when you felt a physical sensation connected to a place or person? What happened?
- When do you feel the most connected to yourself?
- How can you best calm your mind and feel present to your physical sensations?
- Do you remember a time when you trusted your intuition on something and it turned out to be the best decision you could have made?

PRINCIPLE 6: LOVE

"I always keep an open heart" is one of the most powerful intentions I've chosen to adopt. I must admit, I don't always succeed, and I'm still learning, but it has had an amazing impact on how I live, love, and evolve.

Keeping your heart open allows you to make brave decisions and live a full life without regrets. It takes courage to live with an open heart and it takes even more courage to keep it open. It's a lot easier to close your heart, especially when there is a possibility that you might get hurt. When you act from fear, you are more likely to close your heart to protect it. When you come from courage, you can choose to keep it open no matter what.

Life gets even richer, more fulfilling, and deeper when you live with an open heart. It will lead you to live boldly and stay in line with your truth.

I've realized that when I live with my heart wide open, my experiences are even more profound, and life feels effortless and synchronistic. Every time I close my heart because of an experience or a story I tell myself, I allow myself to be pulled away from my courage and truth.

A closed heart is an invitation for fears to come and party on their terms. Instead of letting fears dominate the dancefloor, consciously keep your heart open. You will feel awake, vibrant, and tuned in.

LOVE VS. FEAR

There are two major forces that drive most of our behaviors: love and fear.

Emotions rooted in fear are often based upon scarcity and a need to control something that is outside of your control. Fear-driven responses may manifest as frustration, anxiety, jealousy, rudeness, or anger.

Emotions that stem from love are based on abundance, an understanding that life itself is abundant, and not a tit-for-tat game. Love allows you to live with courage and surrender to the unknown. Love-driven responses show up as courage, kindness, generosity, respect, graciousness, tolerance, understanding, thoughtfulness, and compassion.

Making a brave decision becomes easier when you come from love. Learn to surrender to the flow of life, rather than fighting what you can't control.

The first step in embracing the power of love on your journey to living boldly starts with connecting to yourself.

CONNECTION TO YOURSELF

A connection to yourself is the ultimate driver of confidence and courage. You feel safe to live courageously when you feel connected. On the other hand, a sense of disconnection from yourself and your truth brings uncertainty, which leaves room for fear.

When you are connected to yourself, you will make bolder decisions, even if it feels uncomfortable. You will be aware of the kind of people you don't want to spend time with, because you'll feel like your energy is being zapped when you're around them.

When you open your heart and drop into your truth, you will feel a deep sense of connectedness, calmness, and fulfillment. You may also feel more vulnerable and guided.

But how do you open your heart? And how do you keep it open? The heart-opening process might take five minutes, a few days, a few weeks, or a few months. It takes as long as it takes. Start with the intention to keep an open heart.

When your heart is open and energy is flowing through you, you will not only feel more awake, but also more courageous. You'll live without regrets.

One of my favorite ways to open my heart is the heart drop-in technique.

THE HEART DROP-IN

The heart drop-in is an amazing tool you can use anywhere at any time.

This technique reminds me very much of a drop into a wave on a surfboard. When I'm sitting in the ocean waiting for a wave to lift up behind me, I have to make a choice. If I hesitate or don't commit, I will most likely end up getting dumped and tumbled in an ocean washing machine. If I commit to the drop in and paddle into that wave with everything I've got, the wave will pick me up for a smooth take-off: I jump to my feet and glide along a wall of water with joy and a big smile on my face that can last for days.

When you drop into your heart, you'll feel a deeper love for yourself and others. Energy will flow through you, allowing you to live in a place of courage.

A great way to do the heart drop-in is to close your eyes, put your hands on your heart, and imagine energy flowing through it, feeling love and connectedness. Breathe deeply and slowly as you focus on the sensations in your heart. After a few minutes, a sense of calm and peacefulness takes the place of any fear-based emotion. Whenever you are going through a challenging time or feel like you are not living with courage, do the drop-in more frequently. I often put my hand on my heart when I fall asleep, and again when I wake up.

Sometimes when I feel disconnected or hurt, rather than sliding into fears, I put my hand on my heart and repeat a travel tune to myself that feels right for the occasion, like "I always keep my heart open no matter what," or, "The universe always has my back." Find a mantra that works for you and try it on. You'll be surprised at how quickly your state of mind can change with this practice.

You can do this drop-in technique anywhere: sitting on a plane, working in your office, or standing in a queue. As you put your hands on your heart, imagine your heart opening with energy flowing through it, with your eyes closed or open. The intention is more important than how you do it. Whenever I feel off, or like I'm not making courageous decisions, I remind myself to drop back into my heart.

I also use this technique every time I take the stage for a workshop or keynote address. I know that when I deliver a presentation with a deep sense of connection, it will be even more impactful for the audience. Consciously dropping into my heart and delivering content from that space is incredibly authentic, real, and raw.

The drop-in is also very effective after you've received a poop shower. It helps you to wash it off without shutting down or stalling the energy flow.

Humans are infinitely powerful beings. We have the ability to individually and collectively impact others by tapping into our energies and consciousness. I often like to send love and kindness to other people without them even knowing, and I use this same drop-in technique to do so.

A few months ago, one of my dearest friends was going through a very tough time, so I decided to dedicate my daily drop-ins to her. I put my hand on my heart to feel the energy, and I sent it to her heart every night for a few weeks until she was clear of most of the murky water and swimming in a crystal ocean again. She later told me that she felt that love and connectedness when she most needed it. Even if this all sounds woo-woo to you, why not give it a go? Nothing bad will happen if you feel and give a little more love.

If you have someone in your life who needs a bit of extra support, dedicate your drop-ins to them. Or, if you want to be really brave, practice sending love to someone who wronged you. We are all in this together. Positively impacting others will naturally impact you too.

HOW TO TAP INTO AN ABUNDANCE OF ENERGY

Remember: When you keep an open heart, energy can flow through you. Instead of feeling lethargic or heavy, you will feel alive

"Why do you always have so much energy?" people often ask me. "Is it the food you eat? Or the coffee intake? Or some magic energy-boosting remedy?"

It's probably a combination of different factors. I eat healthily and I do love a coffee high every now and then, but I don't take any magic potions (other than salty ocean medicine). The one thing I am sure of is that consciously keeping my heart open results in an abundance of energy. I also notice that when I close it, I can feel a shift in my energy—it feels heavier, almost like someone unplugged my energy source.

I was recently having an unpleasant interaction with a loved one when I felt my heart close. That reaction was unconscious at first, based on a discussion that left both of us deflated. I usually wake up with a lot of energy, but the next morning I felt tired. I wasn't my usual energetic self. Being aware of my own energies, I asked myself why—and realized it had to do with the discussion from the previous night. I had closed my heart because for fear of getting hurt or hurting someone. I came from fear instead of love, which instantly zapped my energy.

Once you are aware of your behavior, you can make the conscious decision to open your heart again. It's not always easy, but it really is a choice. Make the decision to open your heart and see what happens.

Drop into yourself and you will feel a sense of groundedness. The connections you have with yourself and others will be deeper, less needy, less demanding, and more balanced.

From these feelings of groundedness, love, and connectedness, courage can flourish.

LOVE IS NOT A PIE

Love is infinite. Why, then, do we treat love like it's a pie? Like once you've given someone a quarter, there are only three quarters left? There is an abundance of love; it's not in limited supply.

If you approach love with courage, you see love as infinite, and the relationships you form are based on abundance. On the other hand, if you approach love with fear, you will see scarcity and your relationships will trigger emotions that are taking you away from courage, such as jealousy, frustration, or even possessiveness.

We struggle with unconditional love because conditions are what we know. I will love you more if you take the rubbish out on Thursdays. I will love you more if you tell me how much you love me. I will love you only if you love me back. What if we didn't put conditions on our love? What if we just loved unconditionally?

We could get hurt. It's safer to love conditionally and fearfully, guarding our hearts instead of surrendering.

When love is rooted in fear, some of the common emotions that can come up are jealousy, frustration, unworthiness, or anxiety. Jealousy comes from a fear of potential loss, and it's those fears that will make you want to close your heart. Yet, this is the moment in which you should tap into your courage and consciously choose to keep your heart open despite the fears. That's where magic happens.

If your partner behaves in a certain way because of his own

experiences and stories, you might be triggered to react with a fear-based emotion. Closing your heart may be a natural default because it might protect you from possible pain.

What if you loved deeply and kept your heart open despite the pain? What if you loved without conditions? Instead of trying to change someone to suit your agenda, you choose to love them for who they are in all their truth. This doesn't mean you have to accept every behavior. When you know your truth and what you want in a romantic partnership, or any relationship, you might decide to leave relationships that no longer align with your truth. That's OK.

Love more boldly and unconditionally. If your partner is not being kind, can you respond with kindness despite the scars on your heart? Can you love despite the challenges? Can you keep your heart open despite the pain? Yes, you can!

Love courageously and your partner will most likely want to step up too. Lead by example, not by pointing the finger. Let your behavior be guided by *your* truth.

"Being deeply loved by someone gives you strength, while loving someone deeply gives you courage."
—Lao Tzu

Loving deeply gives you courage. And with a brave open heart comes a deep sense of connectedness, fulfillment, and serenity. Loving boldly and sincerely also leads to fulfilling relationships and friendships.

THE OCTOPUS

A great visual for explaining and understanding conscious relationships and deep connections is the octopus. Imagine the octopus with its tentacles: in a "needy" or fear-based relationship, the octopus wraps all of his or her legs around you, trying to hold you tight. But in a relationship based on courage and truth, only some of the tentacles are interlinked, allowing for each individual to function perfectly on their own.

When you feel deeply connected to yourself, not only does everywhere you go feel like home, but you will also be able to connect with others at a deeper, more meaningful level.

Feeling connected to yourself gives you the courage to stay vulnerable with those around you.

When two or more people who are connected to themselves come together, those relationships become so much richer, deeper, and more authentic. It is a connection based on choice, not necessity or neediness. Connections rooted in abundance, love, and courage will help you bring out the best in each other.

FEELING ALL THE FEELS

Humans have this incredible ability to feel a rainbow of emotions, from dark red to bright purple, from deep sadness to incredible joy. You will feel a wide range of emotions on a daily basis, and even more so if you choose to live boldly.

The beauty of living with courage is that you put yourself into situations where you will feel all types of emotions: ecstatic, scared, joyful, nervous, fulfilled, anxious, euphoric, uncertain, and more. Emotions help you evolve as a human being.

Challenging emotions are part of living. The best way to move past a challenging emotion and not let it get stuck in your body or transform into a useless story is to not push it away. It takes courage to sit in an uncomfortable emotion; it is so much easier to run away from it.

When you fight or numb a feeling through willpower, escapism, or any other clever way, that feeling can get stuck and create energy blocks that can later bite you in the bum, without you knowing where the emotional or physical pain is coming from.

Whether you are feeling anger, frustration, heartbreak, disappointment, or sadness, sit in it, feel it, and allow it to come up so it can move past you. It's like a wave in the ocean lifting up right in front of you. You can't stop the wave, but you can allow it to wash past you by diving under it, being nimble, and getting a little bit washed around. Or, you can learn to surf the wave. But if you try to fight it, you will run out of breath very quickly.

Next time you're feeling an emotion you would normally ignore, try to escape from, or fight, try to embrace it instead. It will eventually disappear on its own. But if you ignore your emotions, they will come back even stronger. Ignorance isn't bliss.

While leaving Istanbul on my motorbike, after spending a few incredible days with overseas friends who flew in to create memories and explore the city together, I felt really sad to leave. My first thought was to just go and distract my mind with another party and a few drinks. I reminded myself of this principle. I allowed myself to feel the sadness, rather than pushing it to the back. I rode for a few hours with complete silence in my helmet, swimming in melancholy. After a while, I could feel the veil lift and a sense of gratitude took the place of sadness.

It reminded me of how important it is to feel my emotions instead of avoiding them.

I didn't always have this knowledge, and if there had been a championship competition for avoiding and ignoring negative emotions, I'd probably have taken first place when I was younger! I remember when my dad passed away suddenly. I tried to escape the heartbreak, sadness, and suffering for a long time. At first, I was in denial about his death. Later, instead of letting myself feel the pain, I tried to numb it or ignore it. For a period of time, I lost my zest for life and became more and more reckless, paddling out into bigger waves than I could handle. I felt apathetic, like I just didn't care about anything. My best strategy seemed to be keeping myself busy so I could numb my feelings—I was seeking escape.

None of that worked. Unconsciously, I was doing these things to avoid feeling this deep sadness of losing my dad so unexpectedly. I didn't know how to process or feel these unfamiliar emotions.

This lasted until months later, when sadness, anger, and heartbreak finally became stronger than my attempts to ignore them. I spent many afternoons sitting on the beach, looking out to the ocean, tears running down my face. I finally allowed myself to sit in sadness. I realized I don't always have to be the strong one, that it is OK to be broken.

It's been over ten years since my dad passed, and I occasionally still get overwhelmed by emotions. Knowing what I know now, I allow them to come for a visit without fighting them or trying to ignore them. There is so much beauty in that.

A few years ago on the anniversary of my dad's death, I was sitting in the ocean alone at sunset, looking at the colors in the sky as they changed into different shades of red and purple. Nature painted an incredibly surreal and majestic picture. It literally took my breath away. I missed my dad terribly and my salty tears joined the salty oceanwater. I just sat there, overwhelmed and allowing sadness to take over my being. And then I felt gratitude, serenity, and wonderment.

When you have the courage to live with an open heart, you will feel deeper, richer, and more intense emotions. Life becomes more colorful and its moments even more magical.

TRAVEL TUNES

- I always keep an open heart.
- Love is infinite.
- It's OK to feel a rainbow of emotions.

PIT STOP: THE HEART DROP-IN

For the next thirty days, consciously connect to your heart through the heart drop-in exercise. Every night when you fall asleep and every morning when you wake up, put one or both hands on your heart and breath slowly and deeply. You will feel a sense of calm and connectedness. If you feel your heart close, consciously choose to keep it open. Observe your energy levels as you connect with your heart more.

TRAVEL JOURNAL

Grab your journal and ponder the following questions.

- What would change in your life if you set the intention "I always keep an open heart?"
- When are you most likely to close your heart?
- Do you remember a time or situation when you closed your heart? What happened? How did you feel?
- Are there areas in your life you are approaching from fear instead of love?
- How would your relationships transform if they were based on courage? What would happen if you loved boldly?
- When or where are you fighting your feelings? How can you surrender to your emotions?
- Are your relationships based on love and courage, or on fear?

PRINCIPLE 7: KINDNESS

In the previous chapter, we looked at having the courage to live with an open heart. Kindness is a continuation of this principal. It's a practical application of love.

Acting with kindness and courage creates a positive, self-perpetuating cycle. The two elevate one another. Practice kindness in every area of your life and you will see the whole world become just a little bit more colorful.

> "*Kindness is like snow—it beautifies everything it covers.*"
> —Kahlil Gibran

I've become obsessed with kindness. I believe my fascination with it has positively influenced every aspect of my life and the people around me. Seemingly insignificant acts of kindness can make a huge positive impact. I hope you will join me in spreading more kindness.

Kindness is being considerate no matter the circumstances. It is about caring genuinely and courageously without getting stuck in stories.

Courage enables you to show kindness independent of how people behave. Just like with love, you will have the ability to show kindness even in the face of fear-based behaviors.

On the other hand, when fear is driving your behavior, kindness can become conditional and you might only be kind when you are met with kindness back.

The power of kindness is beyond measure. Kindness is a life philosophy; you don't have to be Mother Teresa to make kindness one of your superpowers.

BE KIND TO YOURSELF

Let's start with you. Without a full cup of kindness for yourself, it is a lot more challenging to share unconditional kindness with those around you.

How do you respond to yourself? Do you find you're often beating yourself up over something? Are you constantly judging and criticizing yourself in your mind? Do you worry and overthink certain things too much? Or do you treat yourself with kindness?

Maybe you didn't do as well as expected on an exam, didn't win the contract you pitched for, or your business isn't growing as fast as you want it to. What thoughts go through your mind when you think about your most painful failures in life or business? How do you respond to your own perceived shortcomings? How do you react when you make a mistake?

Observe how you react and respond. And remember, you may not be able to control the circumstances, but you can always control your response. You can always choose your thoughts and actions. Will you choose kindness?

ALWAYS RESPOND WITH KINDNESS

"Always respond with kindness" is a powerful mantra to adopt. It's interesting to observe both yourself and others when it comes to how you react or respond to a situation or person.

Let's look at the difference between a reaction and a response. A reaction is a quick, impulsive way to deal with something. It often doesn't bring out the best in the parties involved. A response, on the other hand, is more considerate. Rather than reacting, you take the time to come from a place of kindness. Thoughtful responses usually create better outcomes, whether you're working on an important business deal, talking with a loved one, or interacting with a stranger.

Imagine receiving an email that upsets you. If you react immediately, you are more likely to reply in frustration. If you take a few deep breaths and then respond calmly, you'll get to a place where you can move into genuine kindness, often moving others into a more positive place too. You can get really good at this by consciously practicing kindness.

Email communication is a great place to practice responding versus reacting because you can sit there, close your eyes, take a deep breath, count to three (or one thousand), and then respond with kindness.

But what about in person? What about when somebody is attacking you verbally or being rude? It takes a lot more willpower and courage to stay in kindness when you're face-to-face because you can't hide behind a computer screen and do your breathing exercise without looking like a weirdo. When you feel your blood boil, take a deep breath, think about something or someone you love, and respond with as much kindness as you can muster. It's not always easy, but it's worth it.

A few years ago, I was in San Francisco picking up a rental car to drive down to Santa Cruz for a silent retreat. I walked into the rental car office and my heart sank when I saw the huge line of travelers, all waiting for their cars. By the time I reached the front of the line, the lady was very grumpy, which was understandable. I'm sure dealing with tourists can stretch your kindness levels.

As I was completing the paperwork, I asked her what time the Santa Cruz branch closes. She let out a big sigh, then snapped at me, "I don't know."

In my head, I was thinking, "Isn't it your job to find out?" I could feel a little bit of frustration bubbling up. But then I reminded myself that there is absolutely no point in being grumpy about someone else's grumpiness. So I took a deep breath and repeated in my mind, "Always respond with kindness."

I took out my phone, looked up the Santa Cruz branch number, and called them to find out their business hours. I shared that information with the lady with kindness, making sure I didn't sound sarcastic or snarky.

She looked at me and I could see the energy shift from grumpy to relieved right before my eyes. She realized that the world is not against her, that we are in this together.

It was a brief moment, but it was so powerful, leaving both of us better off. And the cool thing about this is that responding with kindness does not take any more effort than responding with unkindness.

The lady, now smiling, handed me the car keys and proudly announced that she had upgraded my car to a bigger one, which I didn't actually want because, coming from Europe, I'm much better with smaller cars (the medium-sized cars in the US are like trucks for a European). But I didn't want to seem ungrateful, so I thanked her for being so kind, grabbed the key, picked up my big fancy car, and even managed to hit the pavement so hard when I stopped for lunch that I got a flat tire. Luckily roadside assistance was able to help!

It takes awareness and courage to respond with kindness when you feel fear. As with any skill, the more you practice unconditional kindness, the easier it will get. Personally, to stay courageous in my responses I like to repeat the mantra "always respond with kindness." It seems to work like magic in most cases.

How will you choose to respond the next time you are faced with fear-fueled emotions? Can you respond with kindness?

THANK YOU FOR BEING KIND

Kindness is not about blindly accepting or excusing others' behaviors. Establish clear boundaries so that you don't let anyone trample all over you in the name of kindness. When you stay in your truth, you will stand up for yourself and others not with aggression, but with firm and graceful kindness.

If you are caught up in fears, you are more prone to be inauthentically kind because you might be worried about how others react or what they think of you, making your choices dependent on others. Base your kindness in courage and expect to be treated kindly. And even if you aren't, have the courage to stay kind.

Whenever you get triggered by someone's behavior, remind yourself to "always respond with kindness," even when your first emotion is frustration, grumpiness, or anger. Watching someone hold their ground gracefully yet firmly is incredibly attractive. I find it one of the most attractive traits in a human. More often than not, your kind response will soften how someone reacts and inspire them to step up too.

HOW TO MOVE TO KINDNESS

It takes courage to stand up for kindness. And as mentioned earlier, it takes even more courage to respond with kindness when you're met with stressful situations.

Even if you don't approve of someone's actions and reactions, you still have a choice in how you want to respond.

Unconditional kindness can be learned. No matter their circumstances or upbringing, every single person has the ability to be kind.

You may think this seems a little too optimistic, and that you just can't do it. I believe without a shadow of a doubt that you are absolutely capable. Let's look at the behaviors and beliefs that will support you in bringing more kindness into your life.

1. PEOPLE ARE DOING THE BEST THEY CAN

One of my favorite beliefs is that "everyone does the best they can with what they have." And that "best" depends on their own experiences and the stories they are telling themselves. Most humans are born with a kind heart that sometimes gets hardened due to painful experiences and disempowering stories.

When you are experiencing a poop shower or someone is behaving in an unkind manner, remember that their behavior most likely has nothing to do with you.

When somebody is being rude without any apparent reason, it can be very easy to draw conclusions about that person and decide that she is just not a nice human. But what if this person was having the worst day of her life, or had just received some horrible news? Your unconditional kindness may positively impact her day and create ripple effects.

The popular break-up line, "it's not you, it's me" applies here. Other people's actions are often driven by their own stories and experiences, and rarely have anything to do with you, unless of course, you're being a jerk on purpose. First rule: don't be a jerk!

Assume that people generally mean well, even if they are behaving questionably. We all have weak moments that we're not proud of. But there is a big difference between *being* a jerk and *acting* like a jerk. Instead of thinking that someone "is a jerk," rephrase it to "he is acting like a jerk." It's not an identity; it's a behavior, and most likely an impermanent one.

The belief that "everyone does the best they can" empowers you to stay kind and leads you to the next way of living: conspiring for the success of others.

2. CONSPIRE FOR PEOPLE'S SUCCESS

While traveling along the Silk Road, I made an observation that touched me deeply. I often got this vibe of "I've got you, you are safe" from total strangers, both men and women. Even though our skin colors and political and religious views couldn't have been more different in most cases, I felt like the people we met along the way were conspiring for our success. I think when traveling on a motorbike you are so vulnerable and exposed to all the elements that people are even more moved to have your back. It cracked my heart wide open and allowed so many memorable moments of humanity to unfold.

When you come from a place of courage and abundance, conspiring for others' success is not even a question—you just do it! It is such a beautiful way to live.

You can apply this on every level, whether it's making someone's job easier, collaborating, or sharing an encouraging smile.

One day, while riding behind Mike along a Turkish highway, I heard his voice through the intercom: "Oh dang, we're getting stopped for a police check!"

"Finally!" I replied cheerfully. "Finally we get to play with Turkish authority!" As per usual, Mike waved me to go ahead so we could use "reverse sexism" to negotiate with the police. I stopped my bike in front of the poker-faced policeman, removed my helmet, and smiled. The policemen muttered "merhaba" (hello in Turkish) and signaled for us to show our passports and bike documents.

I got off the bike and grabbed my documents with a light-hearted, playful smile and an attitude of "I'm here to collaborate and support you in doing your job."

Another police officer was standing next to the first one, casually drinking tea. I looked at him with a big grin and asked playfully, "Chai?" (which means tea in Turkish). His stern face showed a tiny smile, and he asked if I would like some chai. Or at least that's what I interpreted. I nodded happily, and his gestures told us to park the bikes next to the police cars.

Five minutes later we were sitting on the side of the road drinking tea with Turkish police officers who, for a few minutes, forgot about checking cars. It was such a perfect moment of humanity. It felt like we were conspiring for each other's success. When we got on our bikes again to continue the journey, one of them stood in the middle of the road to block the passing traffic so we could ride off safely. There wasn't really any traffic, but it was his way of showing his support.

Conspiring for people's success leads you to live more boldly because you feel safe when you make friends instead of enemies. You have each other's backs.

3. BE THE OBSERVER, NOT THE JUDGER

Finger-pointing, judging, and blaming have become national sports in many countries around the globe. Blame comes from fear and offers zero benefits, other than taking the load off you and putting it onto someone else without resolving anything.

Blaming is giving your power away to something or someone else. It's not conducive to living boldly. So instead of blaming or judging, take a step back and observe the situation so you can respond with kindness.

Being judgement-free is a worthy intention to add to your courage map. How about "I aim to live without judgment, no matter how nuts or out of the ordinary something or someone may seem." As humans, we naturally judge, but you can aim to judge less and be more kind.

4. PICK YOUR FLAVOR

One of Mike's favorite questions on our motorbike trip was: "If this were an ice cream flavor, what would it be?", referring to an emotion, behavior, or situation.

Kindness can come in different flavors too. Remember: if you are feeling worked up, take a few deep breaths until you are ready to choose which flavor of kindness works for you at that moment.

Here is the menu of flavors to choose from:

Stracciatella: Respond with unconditional kindness (stracciatella used to be my favorite ice cream flavor as a kid—it's vanilla with fine chocolate shavings). No hidden agenda, just unconditional kindness, thanks to your courage.

Peanut butter cup: Respond with presence. Sometimes you don't have words, or can't fit any words in when someone is having a go at you. Just be present and let the bad weather pass. That's the only response I was capable of when my mom was reacting from fear; there was no room for a verbal response. And, quite frankly, I didn't know what to say in that moment, so instead I held the space with presence, awareness, and understanding.

Mint chocolate chip: Respond with playfulness. This one is the most challenging one to pull off, as it can come across as not taking the other person seriously, but it can serve to lighten and disarm a situation. The best way to go about it is to use self-deprecation together with kindness. More on playfulness later.

Pick your flavor when it comes time to respond to a difficult situation . . . they're all delicious and perfect in different situations.

5. MEET PEOPLE AT THEIR LEVEL AND THEN LIFT THEM UP

We often fall into the "rescue" trap, where we think we need to save or, even worse, change someone. You can't change people—ever. So don't waste your time trying! People only change and become better versions of themselves when they choose to. It's presumptuous to think that you should or could change someone else.

Meet people where they are by putting yourself in their shoes and acknowledging their challenge. Instead of telling someone what to do, lead by example. Lead with kindness. They will either choose to step up or not. More often than not, you will see people around you step up when you lead with kindness!

Let me give you an example. Let's say someone is screaming at you on the phone because they didn't receive your delivery on time. Instead of screaming back, put yourself in their shoes and acknowledge their frustration—this will take the heat out of the conversation. "I understand how frustrating it can be when deliveries take so long! I am so grateful you let us know so we can work on our processes and make sure this doesn't happen again." Watch the other person's energy shift! People want to be heard, acknowledged, and understood.

Lead by example by staying in kindness no matter their reaction. And if you can't get a word in, just be present and go back to the peanut butter cup ice cream until they've finished their rant. And then you may add some stracciatella.

While on my travels, I got a message from a stranger asking

about our motorcycle routes, as he wanted to do a similar trip. I didn't respond immediately because I didn't have much computer time when we were on the road.

A few days after his first message, a second very grumpy one followed, basically telling me that I am not a nice person. At first it annoyed me. I had never met this guy and didn't feel like getting abused was cool, but I took a deep breath and reminded myself of the stracciatella approach, to respond with unconditional kindness and thought that "he was doing the best he could."

I first acknowledged his frustration about people not responding immediately. Then I explained that since I am on the road, communication is a bit slower than usual. And then I shared my Google Maps with him. I was so tempted to point out that it was not necessary to be rude. But I knew I could do better than that and repeated my mantra, "always respond with kindness."

What followed was him stepping up, owning up to his behavior, apologizing for overreacting, and thanking me for sharing my maps. If I had been preachy, I'm sure his response would have been different. Kindness works wonders!

6. MAKE "ALWAYS RESPOND WITH KINDNESS" A HABIT

Repeat the mantra "always respond with kindness," until it becomes a habit.

While riding my motorbike through Italy with one of my best friends, we had a running joke about this mantra. It started because I kept forgetting my microphone and leaving it outside of the helmet, which meant that my friend couldn't hear me speak through the intercom. So she would sometimes howl "Put your f****** microphone inside the helmet!" and I would whisper back, "Always respond with kindness." It cracked us both up and left us roaring. The next time I was the one being grumpy, my friend would whisper, "Always respond with kindness," and we would instantly both burst into laughter again.

Kindness is a choice! It takes courage to respond with kindness in situations when it would be easier to slip into fear-based reactions.

Kindness is incredibly impactful when it's genuinely unconditional, with no expectation to receive kindness in return. And the more unconditional you become in every area of life, the more empowered you will feel to live boldly.

THE FAIRY DUST

The world needs more kindness. Every single moment of kindness that you share makes the world a slightly better place. Kindness unites strangers. Kindness encourages you to live bold moments every single day.

"Constant kindness can accomplish much. As the sun makes ice melt, kindness causes misunderstanding, mistrust, and hostility to evaporate."
—Albert Schweitzer

It would make me so happy to see you become obsessed with kindness too, and create moments of humanity everywhere you go. Whether you pick unconditional kindness, presence, or playfulness, bring kindness to your every encounter and watch fears evaporate.

Kindness is the fairy dust of life.

TRAVEL TUNES

- I am kind to myself.
- I always respond with kindness.
- I conspire for people's success and they conspire for mine.

PIT STOP: ALWAYS RESPONDING WITH KINDNESS

For the next thirty days (and forever after) aim to always respond with kindness! If you get frustrated, angry, or worked up about something, remind yourself to respond with kindness. Repeat the mantra in your mind until it becomes a habit. Become so good at this that even if you are confronted with negative emotions, you still manage to respond with kindness.

I invite you to become obsessed with kindness and make kindness a habit. It takes conscious practice to reach a level where you can always respond with unattached and unconditional kindness, but it will transform your life!

TRAVEL JOURNAL

Grab your journal and reflect on the following questions.

- When do you struggle to respond with kindness? Do you remember specific times when you didn't manage to stay kind? Do you remember times when you did? What was the outcome?
- Where or with whom do you feel like you could practice more kindness?
- What impact would "always respond with kindness" have on you and your loved ones?
- Where in your life do you want to boldly embrace kindness?
- What does unconditional kindness mean to you?

PRINCIPLE 8: IMPERFECTION

Nothing in life is perfect, but so many of us let striving for perfection hold us back from taking bold action.

The belief that "everything is imperfect" allows you to live boldly. It frees you to make brave decisions and take courageous action, instead of letting fears of not achieving perfection paralyze you.

So often you see people waiting for the "perfect" moment to be courageous: the perfect moment to start something new or finish something old, the perfect moment to step up, the perfect moment to face a difficult conversation, or the perfect moment to pack your bags and go on an adventure you've been dreaming of all your life.

We often use "I'm just waiting for the right moment" as an excuse to not show up and be courageous. But what if the perfect moment never comes? What if right now is the imperfectly perfect moment? How would you act differently if you realized you didn't have to wait for a perfect moment because every moment is imperfectly perfect?

I sometimes ask myself, "What if this was the last moment of my life? Would I be courageous despite the imperfection, or would I wait for more perfection?"

Perfection is an illusion. Make friends with imperfection and you will be able to step into your courage more and more. Be OK with being imperfect; the price of chasing perfection is staying stagnant. The reward for embracing imperfection instead of staying stuck is a life lived fully, a life true to yourself.

Get comfortable with the potential of messing up and making mistakes. Whether you are saying no to an opportunity or yes to an adventure, there is always the possibility you will make a mistake. What if there is no wrong decision? What if there is only perfectly imperfect?

Embrace imperfection and you will be courageous even when it's easier to chicken out. You will stay courageous even when it's uncomfortable. Being OK with being imperfect is a habit, just like living boldly is a habit, and it has nothing to do with settling for less.

It has everything to do with embodying your truth and realizing that you are giving life your best shot.

IMPERFECT IS INTERESTING

> *"Imperfection is beauty, madness is genius, and it's better to be absolutely ridiculous than absolutely boring."*
> —Marilyn Monroe

Imperfection is beautiful, interesting, and exciting. Imperfection gives something character.

Most things in life are imperfect. Look closely at the most beautiful flower. Can you see how imperfect it is? It is the quirks, the uneven shapes, the slightly wonky leaves, and the variously colored petals that make it so interesting.

Or think of someone you adore. It is most likely their imperfections that are endearing and charismatic: the tiny freckle on the right eye, the flattering noise when they laugh, the smile wrinkles around their eyes, or the birthmark on their arm. There is no duplicate of a person. There is no duplicate of you. There is only one unique you, and you are perfectly imperfect.

Your quirks, both external and internal, make you interesting.

I AM IMPERFECT AND THAT'S OK

A while ago, after I got back from a long flight, I drove straight from the airport to the massage place near my home. As I was paying for the massage, the lady at the counter excitedly told me that they have this new laser technology that will get rid of my freckles. I love surfing and being in the ocean, which is why my freckles have multiplied over recent years. I think freckles are cool. They remind me of summer, salty adventures, and the ocean—three of my favorite things. So I politely declined to join her freckle-fighting mission.

My freckles are perfectly flawesome and they are a part of me because of my lifestyle. If I lived in a freezer for most of the year (like my birth country, Switzerland) or spent most of my life indoors, I'd probably have fewer freckles (and also fewer wrinkles!).

The irrational human desire for perfection has the power to enhance the fear of not being good enough, a fear that holds so many people back from truly stepping into courage and living a full life. Trying to be perfect comes from fear. Maybe you compare yourself to others or to an imaginary situation, but that will send you in a downward spiral toward more irrational fears.

Society has become obsessed with perfection, and we often use it as an excuse to not take action. We wait for perfection instead of taking bold, imperfect action. Maybe you've had a desire to write a book, but striving to achieve perfection prevents you from ever starting. Or you've been wanting to tell your parents how much you appreciate them despite your challenging upbringing, but have not found the perfect time to do so. Or you'd love to ask someone out for dinner, but have not come up with the perfect approach. So instead of courageously taking imperfect action, you are left in perfect inaction.

Redefine what perfect means for you according to your own values, views, and beliefs—*not* someone else's. When you know that you are imperfect, and so is everyone else, you won't be quite as scared to fail. You'll learn to take imperfect action courageously.

It takes courage to confidently embrace your flaws and be comfortable in the imperfect. When you do, your imperfection becomes even more attractive and magnetic!

IMPERFECT IS MEMORABLE

Often when I deliver keynote addresses, I leave a little bit of room for imperfection. I know I will have my audience on the edge of their seats if I walk that fine line between perfection and imperfection. It makes the keynote less predictable and keeps it fresh (rather than polished and rehearsed). It also keeps me on my toes.

This does not mean that I don't prepare. I arrive fully prepared and with an intention of what I want the audience to walk away with. But rather than rehearsing every single word and trying to be perfect, my aim is to be human, real, and imperfect.

When you adopt the belief that you are imperfect and that it's ok, you don't need to wait to be courageous. Take courageous action right now, in the perfectly imperfect moment.

You are not perfect, so get ready to fail!

FAIL

I fail. A lot. And I like it . . . sometimes! Not in a masochistic kind of way of course, but because it is the "failures" that teach me the most and help me to evolve. The mistakes you make support you in becoming better today than you were yesterday. They are your greatest teachers.

If you never make a mistake, you are playing too safe. Living boldly comes with failing and getting back up over and over again!

If you want to step into courage, you must be willing to take risks that have the potential to bring on failure. Be grateful for the many lessons that have come, and are yet to come, with making mistakes.

Don't stay safe. Invite imperfection. And beware of the comparison trap.

THE COMPARISON TRAP

Why have we become so obsessed with trying to be perfect, look perfect, and act perfectly? A lot of this obsession with perfectionism stems from continuously comparing ourselves with others, thereby allowing a very demanding, irrational inner critic to emerge. This obsession fosters the fear of not being good enough, rather than the courage to stay true to yourself.

With social media and the ability to constantly check on what others are doing, people are even more prone to comparison. It's not healthy, and it can leave you feeling like you are not achieving as much as you should. Or, it could make you want stuff just for the sake of it or because of what 'others' are doing, being, or having, and not because it's a desire from your heart.

Comparison puts doubt in your mind and pushes you away from living your truth boldly.

COMPETE ONLY WITH YOURSELF

One question I like to ask myself is, "How can I be a better human today than I was yesterday?" This is a question that helps me to live more boldly and in line with my truth. I feel at peace if I know that I'm doing the best I can with my resources and abilities. And on some days, my best is not perfect, but it might be all I've got. I am imperfect and that's OK, as long as I don't let it hold me back from being courageous.

Don't compare yourself with others. Compare yourself with yourself. Focus on beating your own personal best. Ask yourself, "How can I be the best version of myself at this point in my life?"

Set higher standards for yourself, not based on what anyone else is doing or saying, but based on your own circumstances. How can you continue to grow and not let your imperfections stop you from living boldly?

Life isn't a competition. When you realize that we are all in this together, not against each other, you will be OK with making mistakes. Allow your mistakes to teach you lessons and elevate you to new levels of wisdom.

I felt accepted and included everywhere we went along the Silk Road. I never felt judged for my imperfect opinions, skin color, or political views. So many times, I felt touched by this feeling that, at the core, we are all the same. We are in this together.

WE ARE IN THIS TOGETHER

We are all in this together. We truly are. I absolutely adore this concept. When you come to adopt this belief, you will automatically be more accepting of yourself and others. You will choose kindness and compassion despite your imperfections.

Along our journey many kind humans shared moments of humanity with us, moments I will cherish forever. I remember when we entered Tajikistan from Uzbekistan and realized that we got our visa dates wrong. We were at the border two days too early. The border official looked at our papers and announced sternly that we had to go back to Uzbekistan and come back in two days. Except we couldn't go back due to Mike's Uzbek visa, which granted him only a single entry into the country. With a sinking heart and a nervous smile, armed with Google Translate, I tried to explain the situation. One of the officials waved us to come "backstage" to sort out our dilemma. It was a cold and rainy day, so sitting on a comfy bed in a heated room and sharing snacks with border control wasn't too bad! It took a few hours, many phone calls, sign language, and a few kind strangers to solve the challenge. We ended up getting new visas issued thanks to a local travel agent. The entire experience felt like we were all in this together.

I'm forever grateful for those treasured moments of humanity.

Another brief moment of "we are all in this together" that made me smile was when I pulled up at a toll gate on a highway in Turkey. With sweaty eyelids (I didn't even know this was a thing until I started riding motorbikes in hot temperatures!), I took my helmet off for a quick breather and the woman in the booth let out a surprised "Wow, so good!" in her big Turkish accent when she saw a woman on a bike. We enjoyed sharing a few giggles and exchanging compliments. It enriched both of our days! Had she or I been intimidated, compared ourselves, or let insecurities drive our behaviors, we would have missed out on this perfect moment of humanity. Don't let your fears cause you to miss out on magic moments with strangers. We are all perfectly imperfect and we are all in this together.

PERFECTION IN TINY MOMENTS

My favorite answer to most things is "that's perfect"—whether a friend is making dinner suggestions, my partner is booking a weekend away, or my brother is picking a movie to watch together. It's perfect.

Could it be better? Probably. But right now, it's perfect! There is perfection in tiny moments, or what I like to call momentary perfection. Perfection is in the process, not the outcome.

I sometimes observe people struggling to accept a suggestion, such as a restaurant or holiday destination, because they're fearful that it isn't the perfect option, or that there might be a better one. This may leave the other person feeling deflated and less eager to make suggestions in the future, or even teach them to stop being proactive. Instead of saying no, why not find perfection in tiny moments? Someone making a suggestion in the first place is perfect. And when you manage to go with the flow (and your loved ones' suggestions!), you will experience so much more momentary perfection.

Even in business, I often find myself saying "it's perfect," for now . . . until we have a better solution. Momentary perfection ensures that we keep taking courageous action and moving forward, rather than staying stuck. I know that if we have that attitude, we get stuff done. We don't procrastinate and wait with the pretext because "it's not perfect yet." We launch, we take action, we test, we fall over, we get back up, we learn, we improve, and we go again. When you come from a place of courage, you are not scared of falling over. You are OK with falling over, redoing, and rebuilding because it evolves and elevates you and those around you. You take imperfect action rather than perfect inaction. In this way, you gain momentum and adjust along the journey.

Embracing imperfection doesn't mean settling for mediocrity. I'm a big fan of continuous improvement. In fact, I believe that is one of my primary roles in my businesses: to continuously improve on everything we do. To not settle or get lazy. Learn to see perfection in tiny moments and you will keep evolving and taking bold action.

Embracing imperfection is a journey. And the reward is living fully, courageously, and open-mindedly.

You are imperfect and that's OK. We all are!

TRAVEL TUNES

- I am imperfect and that's OK.
- Imperfect is interesting, beautiful, and authentic.
- There is perfection in tiny moments.

PIT STOP: CELEBRATING MOMENTARY PERFECTION

For the next thirty days, focus on momentary perfection by accepting perfection in tiny moments, rather than continuously striving for more and more.

When a friend is making a suggestion, respond with "that's perfect." Find enjoyment in the perfectly imperfect moments.

TRAVEL JOURNAL

Grab your journal and ponder the following questions:

- What brave decision would you make if you knew that the perfectly imperfect moment is right now?
- Who or what are you comparing yourself to? How does it make you feel?
- How can you be a better human today than you were yesterday?

- What imperfect action could you take to get closer to living boldly?
- Where in your life do you feel like the belief of not being good enough is holding you back from living boldly?
- What courageous decision would you make if you weren't scared of failure?
- How would the belief "we are all in this together" change the way you interact with others?

PRINCIPLE 9: NON-ATTACHMENT

Non-attachment is one of the most powerful and challenging principles when it comes to living courageously. When you master non-attachment, your decisions and actions will no longer be tied to a certain outcome. As you stop worrying about the outcome and start focusing on the present moment, you will be guided by courage instead of fear. Letting go of a desired outcome is so powerful because it leaves very little room for fear to emerge.

> *"Without desire there is stillness, and the world settles by itself."*
> —Lao Tzu

It is natural to have desires, so there is no point in fighting them. However, when you can detach yourself from desire, you will be able to make decisions based in courage. You know that the outcome will be exactly what it is meant to be. Whether you think it's good or bad, it is what it is. The world settles by itself. And remember, the universe always has your back!

THE POWER OF NON-ATTACHMENT

Non-attachment doesn't mean not trying. And it's certainly not about being ignorant or avoidant, either.

I first heard about the principle many years ago when I was sitting in a lecture at a meditation retreat. One of the teachers started talking about detachment. It jerked me out of my daydreaming. (Busted! Guilty of not being completely present at a meditation retreat.) The concept instantly resonated with me on a deep level.

Attachment can come in different versions: attachment to your possessions, emotions, relationships, ideas, results, or thoughts. Attachment is at the center of so many fear-driven emotions, like jealousy, anger, hurt, disappointment, and irritation. For example, the attachment to a certain outcome in a relationship can cause jealousy, neediness, or a feeling of unworthiness. The attachment to possessions can manifest as greed, entitlement, or an irrational fear of loss.

Practicing detachment has nothing to do with being indifferent or unemotional. It's about letting go of something you can't control. You can only control your own choices, behaviors, and actions. You can't control future events.

Once you detach from a desired outcome, once you stop worrying about potentially losing something or someone, once you let go of control, once you surrender, this incredible feeling of freedom will take the place of fear.

Detachment leads you to live every moment courageously and to its fullest without worrying about what's going to happen in the future or what happened in the past. Realize that your happiness or fulfillment doesn't depend on external things or people. Detachment allows you to embrace uncertainty with a brave, open heart. It enables you to have a playful attitude toward life. And ultimately, it allows you to step into your courage—all the way in.

"Detachment is not that you should own nothing, but that nothing should own you."
—Ali Ibn Abi Talib

I've been challenging myself to detach more from material things because I know that, as much as it's nice to have stuff, it's not the stuff you own that supports you in living your best life.

To be honest, I have a long way to go, and I'm definitely not detached from everything I own or experience, but I am intentional about practicing detachment. Some days are easier than others. Many times, I fall prey to the desires and expectations of myself and others.

A few years ago, I was having breakfast with a friend at a local cafe when a gorgeous woman walked over to my table and asked me where I got my jacket. I had bought it on a trip to New York City. I didn't really feel any emotional connection to the jacket, so I decided to give it to her. Her happiness over the gift was far greater than mine for owning it. I admit I did have a moment of attachment and "am I going to miss this jacket?" but concluded that I wouldn't. Her joy and gratitude were priceless. Would I have been able to give away my favorite blue leather jacket if someone asked for it? Nope! I am totally attached to it. I'm a forever student of non-attachment.

Another time, I walked into a coffee shop near my house, wearing a t-shirt with a picture of Seattle's famous Mt. Rainier printed on it. The lady at the counter was so excited to tell me that it was her home mountain. I asked if she'd love my t-shirt and her eyes widened when I took it off and gave it to her. Don't worry, it was summer, and I was wearing a bikini underneath, with my place just a skip away. About a year later, I was running a brand strategy session for that same cafe, and the Seattle lady was sitting opposite me in the offices. We both burst out laughing when we recognized each other. (This time I didn't take my clothes off!)

This all sounds very Zen, but in all honesty, in both cases, the jacket and t-shirt were not my favorite items in my wardrobe. That, of course, made it so much easier for me to detach.

After the last leg of our motorbike journey, on my way back to Sydney from Tbilisi, I forgot that I had four small Swiss Victorinox knives in my hand luggage. I brought them to give to strangers along the way or to use as bribes if we got into trouble (they make incredibly great bribes with policemen!).

Unfortunately, they ended up in the trash can at customs, as I had forgotten them in my hand luggage. I was grumpy for about fifteen minutes, coming up with all sorts of "what if" scenarios in my mind. *What if I had left them with my bike, what if I had remembered to give them to people who would have appreciated them, what if I had them in my checked luggage, what if the customs official would buy into my many excuses* . . . there was no point in what if-ing, yet my mind still needed a few minutes to detach and get over it.

It took a little longer to get over the "breaking of the drone" episode at the border crossing into Uzbekistan. We were on our way from Turkmenistan to Uzbekistan when we were told that no drones were allowed into the country. A few custom officials took pity on us and tried to convince the more rules-driven ones to make an exception and put a lock on our bag so we wouldn't use the drone. Three hours later, a lot of confusion and no solution in sight, one poker-faced customs lady told us we needed to go back to neutral ground and break the drone into pieces. A very apologetic guy walked us back to the neutral zone between Turkmenistan and Uzbekistan to watch us break the drone. He then threw the pieces in all directions and left them there. It all seemed so nonsensical. I was grumpy and struggled a few extra minutes to detach from the unexpected outcome. It was easier to give my shirt away!

THE 3 STEPS TO NON-ATTACHMENT

Here are three steps for practicing non-attachment. These can be applied to detachment from outcomes, people, thoughts, objects, emotions, experiences, or circumstances.

1. FIND CLARITY

First, understand what you want by having clarity in your vision, intentions, and goals. Know your truth and own it.

2. COMMIT

Next, pour your entire soul into whatever you are doing, whether that is your job, a relationship, an adventure, a hobby, or a way of being. You might as well give life your best shot while you are at it. For example, you have chosen to live boldly and now you are giving it your all by reading this book, applying the principles, making brave decisions, making mistakes, getting back up, evolving, and being courageous.

3. DETACH

Lastly, detach from the outcome, because ultimately only you can influence your own behavior. You can't control how the economy is going, whether the sun will be shining tomorrow, or how someone will respond. However, you can always choose your own decisions and actions.

You are doing the best you can with what you've got right now! Be OK with the level of courage you are currently at. You are on your path to living more boldly by being intentional about it. Courage is a journey.

UNMET EXPECTATIONS

Unmet expectations often lead to fear-based thoughts, emotions, and behaviors. Fear may raise her head because of an attachment to a certain expectation.

You may secretly expect your best friend to give a speech at your fiftieth birthday party, and when he doesn't because of his fear of public speaking, you may feel disappointment or resentment—an unmet expectation awakening fears.

Or you may be expecting your partner to buy you flowers on your anniversary, and when he doesn't, you may get trapped in the fear of not being loved.

Our journey along the Silk Road reminded me to let go of expectations in order to enjoy the present moment. Day by day I was invited (or forced) to let go of my expectations. I remember one particular afternoon in Kyrgyzstan: It was already quite late in the day and, according to Google Maps, we were hours away from our accommodation. Feeling tired, hungry, and cold, the prospect of a warm shower and food was very enticing, so we pushed on. What we and Google Maps didn't know was that the roads were about to get a lot worse. Because of the considerably slower speed we were traveling, the three hours turned into five, then eight, then fifteen! It was evident that we would never make it to our accommodation unless we wanted to ride all night, which would have been too dangerous on those roads. Since we were in the middle of nowhere without any civilization in sight, I suggested that we ride until sunset and then pitch our tents. Once I let go of my expectation of how I would spend the night (fed, showered, and tucked in!), I went from rushing and hardly enjoying the scenery to enjoying the muddy journey and the beauty of nature surrounding us. It was such an impactful shift. We ended up spending the night next to a few yurts with local kids who followed our every move with astonishment in their eyes as we set up our tents. We didn't shower or eat, and we froze our buns off during the night. But it was one of the most memorable experiences. Waking up surrounded by mountains and cows grazing in front of our tents was pretty special!

Having an attachment to the outcome is giving your power away. You can't control the circumstances or other people's behaviors, but you can choose how you respond. I couldn't control the road conditions, but I could choose how I wanted to act and ultimately feel about the experience. Serenity and unexpected beauty followed, thanks to letting go of expectations and surrendering to the present moment.

When you have clarity about who you are, honor what you stand for, and act with integrity, it will be easier to trust in the process and detach from the outcome, even if the outcome is an unmet expectation.

Your happiness and level of contentment very much depend on your own expectations. When you can let go of them, it's almost impossible not to feel fulfilled. The more you let go of expectations, the more you will find calm, joy, bliss, and contentment.

DON'T BE AFRAID TO LOSE EVERYTHING

Let's play with this principle and take it to a whole new level!

Most things in life are impermanent. Your emotions, mind, body, career, relationships—they all continuously change and evolve into different forms. Yet most of us are resistant to change. Change is unpredictable and can feel uncomfortable. We hold on to things, even if they don't serve us anymore, due to a variety of fears.

What if you lost everything today—your home, your relationship, your business, your possessions—would you be OK? Would you survive? Would you recover?

Play with that thought for a minute. It's something I've thought about quite a lot on my journey toward non-attachment. If you can detach from your desires and get to a place where you know that you'd be OK if you lost everything, you'll have more freedom to live your life courageously.

When you get to a point in your life where you are at peace and have an inner knowledge that you would be OK no matter what, your decisions won't be driven by fear anymore.

What decisions would you make if you knew that you'd be OK no matter what happened? What actions would you take? What would you change? Where in your life would you step up?

Speaking of stepping up, let's look at one of the most beautiful human virtues powered by non-attachment to a response or outcome—unconditional generosity.

UNCONDITIONAL GENEROSITY

After spending hours on bumpy off-roads through the most stunning Georgian landscapes, Mike and I stopped in front of a tiny wooden stall on top of a mountain pass. A middle-aged man was selling homemade treats. I felt my stomach rumble, so I bought something that looked like a cookie. We sat down next to his stall, overlooking the valley below us to take in the views.

After a few minutes, the man brought fresh bread, tomatoes, and cheese in a bag, pointing at the cow grazing next to us: the cheese was from her. This was as "farm to table" as it gets. He sat next to us, silently smoking a cigarette with a big smile on his face, happy to see us devour his unconditional gift. There was zero expectation or attachment to any outcome; he just wanted to share his food. He was enjoying a precious moment with strangers. I may have ruined it a little by offering money he wouldn't accept.

Another time, when we were riding along the famous Pamir Highway in Tajikistan, my bike got a flat tire. All those bumpy off-roads had taken a toll on King Giorgio's feet! Mike's mechanical skills came in handy when we were stranded in the breath-taking Pamir mountains at 4,000 meters above sea level. In the hour it took to fix the tire, four trucks drove past, and every single one of them stopped to offer help. One truck driver handed us a fresh loaf of bread and walnuts out of his window! We enjoyed a welcome picnic on the side of the road with stunning views of the snow-capped mountains thanks to his generosity.

Unconditional giving with no expectations and zero attachment to an outcome truly makes the world go around.

Why, then, are we so used to being conditional with generosity? Or with love and kindness? Why do we so often expect a certain outcome and get upset if it doesn't happen the way we expected? Because that's how we're used to living. But there is another way. Why not change this habit and strive to be unconditional? Instead of staying stuck in your expectations, come from courage and give love and kindness unconditionally.

How can you integrate more unconditional giving into your life? Don't expect a return when you do something nice. A great way to practice this is to be generous with people who won't be able to reciprocate.

Life is not a tit for tat game. Life is abundant. Give it your best shot, let go of expectations, and then detach from the outcome.

I MISS KING GIORGIO

On our last motorbike ride through Tbilisi in Georgia, I felt a wave of sadness overcome me. I knew I would miss the daily adventures on my motorbike. "Screw detachment," I laughed through the intercom to Mike. "I'm going to miss King Giorgio. My heart feels heavy!" And off we went laughing and making fun of my attachment issues.

As much as we can practice detachment and improve, there will be times where you will miss your very own King Giorgio, and that's OK. Allow for the emotions that attachment brings to pass through you, rather than fighting them or getting upset about feeling attached to something or someone. It's natural. Detach from feeling attached!

You will get better at non-attachment by being aware and reminding yourself of this principle every single day. I still fall into attachment—a lot! When I catch myself running that same old pattern, I observe my thoughts, feelings, and behaviors, and then try to shift. Sometimes it's easy, sometimes it's more challenging. Instead of getting upset about not being able to detach, I detach from my unmet expectations and allow myself to be OK with where I'm at and what I'm feeling.

It takes courage to practice non-attachment consistently. The more you detach, the more your decisions will be guided by courage instead of fear. Come back to this chapter whenever you need a reminder.

Know that even if you lost everything, you'd be OK. We are all in this together. And remember, the universe always has your back, even when it doesn't seem like it.

TRAVEL TUNES

- If I lost everything, I'd be ok.
- I give life my all and I detach from outcomes.
- I got this. I am capable of handling anything life throws at me.

PIT STOP: WHAT IF YOU LOST EVERYTHING?

Play with the thought of "what if you lost everything" until you get comfortable with it, until you feel that you would be OK if you did. Visualize and imagine losing everything that you're attached to. Put yourself in that place, and find out for yourself: would you be OK? Could you handle it? Would you rise from the ashes? I bet you would!

TRAVEL JOURNAL

Get your journal and reflect on the following questions:

- What courageous decisions would you make if you weren't attached to a certain outcome?
- What are you feeling most attached to in life right now?
- Where do you feel like attachment is holding you back from living with courage? What do you need to let go of?
- In which area of your life would you most like to practice detachment? What is the first step you can take toward non-attachment?

PRINCIPLE 10: FLOW

Flow with life gracefully and let its currents carry you to the most magical, mystical, and mysterious places. Trust the flow of life instead of resisting it and you will live from a place of courage.

When you embrace flow, you are less likely to make room for fears because even if things don't work out the way you'd like them to, you can course-correct around any obstacle, just like the flow of water. Don't fight life's flow—dance with it gracefully.

ADAPTABILITY IS YOUR SECRET POWER

"It is not the strongest of the species that survives, nor the most intelligent that survives. It is the one that is most adaptable to change."
—Charles Darwin

This principle supports you in being more adaptable. Adaptability is a virtue that allows you to navigate through life with ease. In fact, adaptability is one of the most important skills in today's fast-paced world. The speed at which societies are changing is accelerating. For people struggling to adapt, change can bring a multitude of fears.

When you are able to flow and adapt easily, you will see abundance and the potential to move humanity forward. Choose to see opportunities to change, adapt, lead, and evolve to the next level.

If you let fears dominate your life, you will often have the sensation of banging your head against a wall, because you are holding on to a plan that makes you feel safe. Staying stuck in fear will make you struggle to adapt to new places, people, or situations.

On my motorbike adventure around the world, I wanted to embrace and test this concept of flow and adaptability, allowing the journey to guide me without big plans. My intention was to put this principle to work and see if it would enable me to approach the trip with more courage. I wanted to have enough room for unpredictability. We created a rough plan with enough flexibility for someone or something to come along and take us off our planned route because there might be something interesting to see or do that we didn't even know about while planning our trip. This led to many synchronistic moments and unforgettable experiences.

One fine morning in Georgia, we decided to spend the day riding off the beaten track, exploring the picturesque trails over a mountain pass.

Darkness was falling, and we were still miles away from the town where we were aiming to spend the night. We were both exhausted from all the bumpy roads, so instead of making it to our destination, we pulled into the next village and found a cute boutique hotel. After a quick shower, we met in the lobby bar for dinner and some self-guided Georgian wine tasting.

Well, it turned out the kitchen was closed, but the wine was flowing. So we ordered two glasses of each wine on the menu followed by a few more, and ended up with the hotel owner and a few of his friends sitting around us in the courtyard, as they shared local wine and offered us tips on places to explore in the area. Sign language and images on the phone worked perfectly since we didn't speak Georgian. Our Georgian and their English improved as we tasted more wine.

The owner told us about this ancient cave monastery on the side of a mountain about an hour from the hotel, in the opposite direction from where we were heading. The next day, we ditched our plans and headed to the monastery. It was one of the most magical rides and days of our entire journey (despite the hangover).

Some of the deepest and most unexpected experiences in my life have happened because I abandoned my original plan.

"You can't stop the waves, but you can learn to surf."
—Jon Kabat-Zinn

I love this metaphor of surfing the waves of life. Waves are powerful; the more you fight them, the longer you will stay under water and the faster you will run out of breath. Instead, you can learn to surf. Suddenly, what seemed like an obstacle becomes your best friend in reaching a peak performance or bliss state. If you don't want to learn to surf literally or metaphorically, you can also let your body go all floppy while the wave washes over you and tumbles you around. You will come up for air a lot more quickly than by fighting the undercurrents of a wave.

FLOW LIKE WATER

No natural river is arranged in a perfectly straight line. Every river has twists and turns. Life is not a straight line either; on your life's journey, there will be many unexpected crossroads.

When you encounter an obstacle, imagine being like the water that flows around the rocks. Don't fight them or pretend they are not there, but find a different path so you can move past them. Sometimes adjusting will be effortless, and sometimes you'll get stuck behind a rock until you can flow freely again.

Remind yourself of this analogy whenever you hit a challenge or get stuck in a current. If you fight the current, you are more likely to run out of steam.

When you approach big decisions with flow, you are more likely to take the path that is the most authentic one for you. You will take bold action and trust that the details usually work themselves out along the way. Some doors may not open for you because they are either not your doors, or because you just need to come back with a different key or approach. Trust your intuition to know when to push and when to let go.

During my studies at Geneva University, I decided to find a place I could study abroad. I had never been to Australia before and felt a pull to go explore this big island.

So, I applied for a scholarship with Sydney University. After a few interviews and English tests, I got accepted. I was excited and a little nervous. Would I like Australia? I had a feeling that I would. On the flight over, I sat next to a young German woman who made sure I knew about every deadly animal in Australia by the time we landed in Sydney.

I didn't have accommodations or work sorted out when I arrived, as I thought it would be easier to work out the details once I was on the ground. I stayed with a friend for a week and spent the first few days figuring out where I wanted to live. Going with the flow rather than trying to organize everything from Switzerland allowed me to pick a suburb close to a beach I liked.

As for work to finance my studies, I just walked into a bar that looked cool and talked the bar manager into hiring me. It was relatively easy, since they didn't know I had no clue about making cocktails, or that I couldn't distinguish or even pronounce the different beer brands on offer. (Thanks to my kind fellow bartenders for teaching me on the job and always having my back!) I eventually made friends with the DJ and started playing the saxophone in different bars and clubs across town, which was a lot more lucrative than bartending.

My life would be completely different if I hadn't gone with the flow and instead stayed safe in my home environment. Who knows, I might have even married a handsome Swiss farmer and spent my days tending to our cows and riding horses through the forest. Doesn't sound bad at all!

Who knows what tomorrow will bring? When you flow and stay flexible, you don't need to know how everything will work out, because you'll learn to enjoy surfing the waves of life instead of trying to fight them.

EVERYTHING IS IMPERMANENT

Remember, everything is impermanent and nothing remains the same forever. Your surroundings, your life, your opinions, your relationships, your emotions, and your needs—they all continuously change. There is nothing that doesn't change. The more you practice detachment, the more you will flow, and the more you will live courageously.

"Change is the only constant."
—Heraclitus

See change as a welcome evolution, even if it's sometimes tough to handle. Most of the time you end up in a better place after the change, although you might not realize it until later.

Surrendering to change and embracing impermanence allows you to live more courageously because you know that even if things don't work out how you'd like them to, the result is also impermanent. You know that if you are stuck behind an obstacle right now, it's highly unlikely to be your "forever position."

Remember those times when your life momentarily turned into an involuntary obstacle course and you wondered when it was going to end? It might have lasted a few hours, weeks, or months. Maybe you are even in the middle of an obstacle course right now!

Have you ever seen an athlete stand in front of a hurdle screaming "get the f*** out of my way!" or look at a suspended rope yelling "I hate you, stupid rope!"? No! Generally, they give it a go and get on with it. They might fall down and get bruised in the process, but then they get up and keep going.

Yet in life, we sometimes throw tantrums because "It's just not fair!" Well yes, some things don't seem fair—but screaming at the obstacle won't remove it. Embracing the flow will help you dig into your courage so you can move past obstacles with grace.

Know that obstacles are unavoidable and that you will evolve as you navigate around or over them.

"The only way to make sense out of change is to plunge into it, move with it, and join the dance."
—Alan Wilson Watts

THE FLOW SPECTRUM

There are different levels of flow that suit different people. Some people thrive with unpredictability and variety, whereas others prefer a little bit more control and structure. Everyone falls on a spectrum, from loving unpredictability to abiding by structure and certainty.

If you have a low tolerance for unpredictability, then you will want to stay on the side of the flow spectrum with a lot of certainty and control. You will feel better with a stable job, consistent routines, and a detailed plan for your vacations. At this end of the spectrum, you love to be in control and flow may come less naturally.

If this is you and you find yourself pushed all the way to the other side of the spectrum, where it's all flow and unpredictability, you'd feel very uncomfortable and may even freak out sometimes when you get overwhelmed with chaos. Instead of making huge changes all at once, push yourself by adding small elements of flow into your life—such as taking a different route to work, letting your partner select a dinner place without worrying if it's the "right" one, or going on a weekend adventure without fixed plans.

On the other end of the spectrum, if you love variety, unpredictability, and uncertainty, you'll most likely feel at home being an entrepreneur or working a job that is less routine-driven. You're probably OK not knowing where you're going to sleep or eat until you reach your destination, or, if a plan changes, you are comfortable adapting very quickly. You'll be more likely to embrace flow in full throttle.

Many of us fall somewhere in the middle of the spectrum. No matter where you're at, you can practice adding more flow to your life. You alone decide and have the ability to make changes, one tiny step at a time. You will notice that the more you consciously practice flow, the more risk tolerant you will become, which leads to bolder decisions.

Observe your own behaviors and patterns. Are you often trying to control situations, people, or outcomes? Notice when you're being too rigid or get stuck on something, and remind yourself to be flexible and go with the flow.

If you are in a relationship, it's also helpful to know where you and your partner are on the spectrum so you can respect each other's needs. One of you might have the entire week's meal plan worked out, and the other might not make a weekend plan until it's Saturday morning. Knowing each other's flow tolerance can avoid misunderstandings and feelings of frustration.

Regardless of where you land on the spectrum, if you want to live more boldly, you must consciously take action to get more comfortable with flow. Remember that change is inevitable, and flow supports you in staying calm and courageous despite change.

HOW CAN YOU EMBRACE FLOW?

Be OK with whatever your flow tolerance is. The good news is that you can absolutely learn to embrace flow no matter what your past looks like. Here are six practices that will help you adopt more flow and expand your courage boundaries.

1. PUSH GRACEFULLY

Flow doesn't mean that you are just drifting in the sea, waiting for someone to come and save you. If you know your truth, you will recognize when it's time to push gracefully, not forcefully.

For example, imagine you've been in the same job for five years without a promotion. Instead of waiting for your boss to recognize you and offer you a promotion, you might decide to be more proactive, demonstrate your value, and have a discussion with her about opportunities to step up. A little graceful push can go a long way.

I remember sitting at customs on my way into Turkey when we faced a few bureaucratic challenges regarding our motorcycle registrations. Knowing that patience is not (yet) my virtue, I was aware and had already accepted that it might take a lot longer to get our papers sorted than usual, but that we could push gracefully to get the job done. It took a few hours and a ridiculous amount of paperwork. Just when we thought everything was done, the guys in charge all went on a two-hour lunch break before giving us the final stamp. We embraced flow and made friends with the remaining administrators who served us a copious amount of tea. What could have been a painful experience turned into a fun one.

Even when you need to push, you can do so with grace, playfulness, and a touch of flow. Be clear on what you want, but stay fluid as you work to get there. Resorting to grumpiness or disrespect generally doesn't accelerate the solution.

And then there are times when complete surrender is your best friend.

2. SURRENDER AND THEN SURRENDER SOME MORE

Surrendering is flow's best friend. As much as it takes courage to push, it takes even more courage to surrender—to let go of all control and be OK with whatever happens. And when you do, you open the window for courage to come and play.

This reminds me very much of practicing yoga. There are positions my body doesn't want to get into, but the harder I push myself into a twisted pretzel (there are more professional names for these positions), the less my body will go there. However, the more I surrender, the easier it gets.

Sometimes we sabotage our best opportunities because they seem scary or because we don't know all the steps along the way. When you embrace flow, you don't need to know all the steps because you know you will figure them out as you go. Trust in the process. That ability to surrender completely allows you to live more boldly.

We can't stop life's obstacles, but we can learn to surrender, flow, and adapt like chameleons.

3. BE A CHAMELEON

I love "chameleon wisdom." It can help you to adapt and feel comfortable in settings where you'd normally feel awkward or out of place. Just like a chameleon, you can be fluid and adaptable in the way you talk, dress, or behave—without losing yourself. You don't need to compromise who you are. Each of us is incredibly complex, and there are so many different aspects of your personality. Embrace all your colors.

Having the ability to embrace uncertainty supports you in all sorts of scenarios. It can enable you to be at ease in situations where you might normally be uncomfortable or feel like you don't belong.

For example, when I went axe-throwing with my friends, I put on my sneakers instead of heels and let slip an occasional Swiss swear word. When I'm in meetings with high-level CEOs, I tap into my classier side by putting on a dress or jeans with heels and dropping the swearing (I don't wear suits or corporate outfits because that just doesn't feel like me).

To feel at ease in most situations, combine the principle of truth with flow. If you own your truth, you will realize that you already belong right where you are. You belong to yourself. And when you give yourself identity from the inside rather than the outside, you will be able to flow in most settings. Surroundings don't change who you are; only you can change who you are.

Of course, there are places and communities where you might find it harder to use chameleon wisdom to feel at ease. And there are some you might choose to opt out of entirely.

I remember when I was in San Diego and got invited to a fancy business dinner. I put on my favorite heels, skinny jeans, and a black blouse, and was looking forward to meeting like-minded people. Walking into the chic restaurant in downtown San Diego, a quick glance around the room made me realize that there were hardly any other women in attendance.

The dinner was arranged by a global organization that I am a member of. To become a member, you have to run a business that turns over at least seven figures, hence the lower number of female members (something I'm advocating to change!). Initially, I felt like the guys in fancy suits weren't really taking me seriously and were wondering why I was there, thinking I must be the wife of a business owner in attendance. For the first time in a long time, I felt a little bit out of place.

I soon realized that it was my own insecurities talking!

So I decided to change my attitude and my self-talk. I consciously owned my truth, embraced flow, kept my heart open, and stopped trying to fit in. I let go of the judgments in my head, and what followed were stimulating discussions, shared business insights, and new friendships.

Let go of the need to be liked or to fit in and embrace flow instead. Being a chameleon doesn't mean letting go of your authentic self. In fact, it is the opposite: you are so at ease with who you are that it allows you to courageously flow and find enjoyment in most situations. (And if you don't enjoy yourself, there is always a mic drop and exit option!)

4. EMBRACE OPTION B

I love what Sheryl Sandberg, COO of Facebook, suggested when she was going through the toughest of times. "Option A is not available. So let's kick the shit out of Option B." It is such a great principle to live by.

It's very possible that Option A will not work out. Instead of getting upset about it or throwing a tantrum, why not course-correct, flow, and come up with Option B?

And when you do, go all in! Give Option B your best shot! Sometimes you see people come up with another option but, because they are still attached to Option A, they only give it half their energy.

And if Option B doesn't work, well, there is always Option C. Luckily the Roman alphabet has twenty-six letters!

I got tested on this concept when I rode my bike to the border of Iran. My dream was coming true as the customs officials stamped my visa paper, and with a big smile proclaimed, "Welcome to Iran!" I had been excited about visiting this country for years, and I had finally made it!

A few days earlier Mike and I split ways because it was very challenging to get into Iran with his US passport. He was planning on riding north while I travelled south through Iran, and we were going to meet again in Turkmenistan after two weeks.

With my passport and visa in hand, I felt a bit nervous and excited at the same time. I walked over to my bike, smiling at the customs official who was checking out my bike. Suddenly, he pointed at my plate number and asked me for my bike document a second time. "Problem," he muttered. He said my plate number didn't match up with my bike document.

It turned out that we accidentally put the wrong plate on my bike when we got the bikes ready in Tbilisi. Mike had mine and I had his. As quickly as my dream to ride through Iran came true, it was over. I tried my best persuasion techniques. Nope. There was no chance they would let me into the country with the wrong number plate.

With tears in my eyes I got on my bike and rode back into Armenia. It took three days to get back to Georgia, where Mike was waiting for me, and it took me three days to get over not being able to ride through Iran. Three days! I clearly have not mastered the Principle of Non-attachment! There were split seconds when I considered leaving my bike behind so I could just enter Iran by public transport, which is what one of my Iranian friends suggested. I reminded myself to embrace and kick the crap out of plan B, which was to continue riding my bike by taking another route. I'm glad I did. The adventures that ensued were priceless! And now I'm here sharing some of them with you. To be honest, swapping our plates is such a ridiculous mistake that I sometimes wonder if I was just not meant to travel through Iran alone this time.

Is there an area in your life where Option A just isn't working, even after you've given it your all? What if you doubled down on Option B?

5. SAY GOODBYE TO YOUR INNER CONTROL FREAK

Humans have different levels of control freakiness inside of them. Some are off the charts. The need for obsessive control usually comes from fear. Control feels safe because it seems like you are in charge. Apply the principle of trust and you will learn to stop trying to control situations and other people.

If you are serious about living more boldly, then don't take your inner control freak so seriously. Learn to flow more.

6. BE PRESENT

When you let go of control, you can savor each moment, instead of worrying about the next or the previous one. Flow allows you to be present and find enjoyment in tiny moments.

Let's say you are stranded at an airport due to flight delays. Instead of going nuts because your plans are being messed with, you can choose to enjoy the present moment. Learn to enjoy the moments with a stranger or by sipping on your favorite drink while catching up on work. There isn't much you can do about the flight delays, which are outside of your control. But you can choose what you do and how you feel about it. Stay present, rather than stressing out about something you can't change.

Be OK with where you are on the flow spectrum right now. Remember that being courageous is a journey, and it is one defined by you.

Let the flow of life lead you to magical moments and places, even when things are not going exactly the way you'd like them to. Even when you are experiencing the worst day ever, know that nothing lasts forever. Surrender, and then surrender some more. Know your destination, but be fluid about how you get there. And sometimes you may decide to change your destination. Plunge into flow and your decisions will be guided by courage instead of fear.

I invite you to dance with life. Surrender and surf the wild, raw, and beautifully powerful waves of life.

TRAVEL TUNES

- Everything is impermanent.
- I flow like water.
- I surrender and then I surrender some more.

PIT STOP: THE FLOW SPECTRUM

Play with the flow spectrum by consciously surrendering to life more often. Rather than planning every detail of your next adventure, leave room for spontaneity. Or when choosing a dinner place, just go with the flow and pick a new place you feel drawn to. Embrace going with the flow and enjoy the new encounters and experiences as you do.

TRAVEL JOURNAL

Grab your journal and reflect on the following questions.

- How would your life change if you embraced flow? What would happen if you surrendered more?
- How can you tap into the power of adaptability? In what areas would you like to be more adaptable?
- What courageous decision would you make if you knew that everything was impermanent?
- How would flow support you in living boldly?
- Where do you feel like you need to let go of control? Where do you want to learn to let go of control?
- When does your inner control freak dictate your behaviors?
- Do you remember a time when chameleon wisdom came in handy? What happened?

PRINCIPLE 11: PLAYFULNESS

Playfulness is a subtle art that can soften difficult decisions, conversations, and actions that require courage.

An attitude of playfulness enables you to bring a level of lightheartedness to even the most difficult situations. This lightheartedness takes the edge off circumstances or decisions that might otherwise scare you. It invites courage to play. Whenever faced with a challenge, instead of having a drink to take the edge off, try a shot of playfulness!

Approaching life with a pinch of playfulness can make most experiences less heavy and more digestible. Playfulness has the incredible power to disarm even the darkest of moods or circumstances.

At a few of the border crossings on our motorcycle journey, we sometimes got a bit nervous, because you just never know what to expect. Mike would usually wave me ahead to talk with the border control. It gave me so many great opportunities to test this principle of playfulness, and to witness the positive impact it has on me and those around me.

It was interesting to see how playfulness enables courage and improves many situations for everyone involved. A playful approach has the power to make someone in the grumpiest of moods smile. Just like when we got stopped by the notoriously strict Turkish police and ended up drinking tea on the side of the road. Or the poker-faced border control official who cracked a smile when I offered him Swiss chocolate.

Playfulness brings light to darkness and opens the door to courage.

"Humanity has advanced, when it has advanced, not because it has been sober, responsible, and cautious, but because it has been playful, rebellious, and immature."

—Tom Robbins

LIFE IS YOUR PLAYGROUND

When our basic needs are met—when we have food, shelter, and clothing, and no predators are chasing us—what do we do? We play.

Play is an evolved part of the human experience. As children, we get this intuitively. As adults, we sometimes forget.

Play tends to be the first thing that gets shut down or lost when fear or stress overrides our lives. Many of us simply forget how to play as we take on more of life's responsibilities. We forget that life is like a big playground, so we come up with so many excuses as to why we can't do the things that used to light us up—too much work, too many commitments, too many responsibilities, too much busyness, too many excuses, too many fears.

A playful attitude toward living will not only quash fears, but it will also encourage you to make room for more of the activities you used to enjoy and the people that bring you joy.

Playfulness keeps your mind curious. Curiosity is such a wonderful instigator of courage. Children are a great example of this. Kids want to explore because they are curious about the world around them. They follow a caterpillar around the garden and ask questions without filters or fears. They are courageous because of their insatiable curiosity and lack of preconceptions.

Playfulness is a subtle art. If playfulness were a country, it would be bordered by silliness on one side and rudeness on the other. If you try to be playful but are scared of being disliked, or you feel too self-conscious, you may find yourself acting silly or rude instead. I'm sure you've observed people who tried so hard to be playful that they missed the mark. Like someone dropping too many inappropriate jokes in the hopes of being funny. Or someone commenting on your outfit at a dinner party in a way that puts you down. His comment may seem rude, even though he was attempting to be playful and break the ice. If done the right way, playfulness will always connect rather than divide.

Being playful is not the same as being funny. Someone being funny may make you laugh, but someone being playful will make you feel included.

Playfulness is graceful, charismatic, and intelligent. Take play seriously!

PLAYFUL BLUNTNESS

We were riding through the Swiss Alps on our way south, toward Italy, when we got caught in traffic at a construction site. A few older bikers on Harley Davidsons joined us in the queue. With curiosity, we started sharing stories from our adventures. When I told them about our plans to ride through Eastern Europe and into Asia, they couldn't help but make a few racist comments. I knew they came from a place of fear and wanted us to be cautious. "That's a bit racist," I blurted with a warm smile and a little nudge. I could see the wheels turn in their minds, and we launched into a lighthearted discussion on our very different viewpoints of cultures and religions.

"How do you get away with so much?" Mike asked the next morning, when we were in gluten heaven with freshly baked Swiss bread, croissants, and honey from the local beehives.

Mike pointed out that I seem to be able to share my thoughts with people in a very direct, unfiltered, and blunt way without causing drama and without hurting or offending anyone. I had never really thought about it until then.

I was on my second coffee and could feel the caffeine high coming as we dove into a discussion on courage and playfulness, down the rabbit hole, at double speed.

As I was reflecting on bluntness, an idea dawned on me. I pulled out my notebook and wrote down two words: "Playful + blunt."

That's how you can get away with things that could otherwise fall on closed ears or get you into trouble: getting the message across in a very direct yet playful way, without wrapping it in cotton wool or being dishonest. You can be playfully blunt in a way that is polite and not insulting, kind and not arrogant. Bluntness alone can hit a wall, stir up fear-based emotions, or be perceived as rude.

A message or thought delivered in a playful way is often more welcome, heard, and understood. You are expressing yourself in a way that lets others know you are not perfect either. You are inclusive, and not positioning yourself or your opinions above theirs.

Next time you need to deliver a blunt message, remember to deliver it with playfulness. Do it with a smile, open your heart without judgment, and let them know that you are not perfect either. We're all in this together.

Playfulness has this almost magical power to disarm people instantly. It's nearly impossible to resist playfulness. Playful words and actions bring a level of innocence and can be endearing as long as your intentions are pure.

SEVEN WAYS TO BE MORE PLAYFUL

Speaking in front of larger audiences provides a great playground for me. It's a place where I can apply and test different levels of playfulness, as I'm never quite sure how the audience will respond. I love engaging my audiences with playfulness.

After doing a keynote address on the topic of team culture at a conference in Los Angeles, one of the attendees approached me with an inquisitive look on his face and asked, "How can I be more playful?" At this particular event, the audience had been very warm and receptive to playfulness, so I got to be extra playful and fluid in the delivery of the content.

It was a great question, and one I wanted to think about so I could give him a helpful answer. He wanted exact strategies. I asked myself, can playfulness be learned or is it something you are born with? You may be born with a certain level of playfulness, but it's a subtle art anyone can learn.

Here are seven approaches to turn up playfulness.

1. DON'T TAKE YOURSELF TOO SERIOUSLY

Self-deprecation, and not taking yourself too seriously, is very endearing and disarming when it comes from a place of sincerity. When you don't take yourself too seriously, you are able to tap into your courage because you are not too worried about what others think of you or about making mistakes.

Point out and embrace your own flaws and imperfections in a humorous, confident way. When you do, you put yourself on the same level as others. It's like saying, "Hey, I'm not perfect either, let's play!" There is no room for patronizing. You are flawesome just like everyone else! Remember that imperfect is interesting and beautiful.

Self-deprecation can also work when you are faced with someone's fear-based reactions. It has the potential to disarm their anger or frustration. Instead of letting your own fears be triggered, respond with playfulness and see what happens.

Early one morning, I was walking to my car when my neighbor stopped me. In a shrill voice, she started to tell me off about the music we had been playing the night before. My friends and I have a band called Salty Lips (don't ask!) and we had had a practice session at my place.

So instead of defending myself, I joined her rant and let her know that I would be a little frustrated too, especially if the music isn't that amazing. She calmed down straight away and went from "Don't ever do this again" to "Maybe just play a few different songs instead of repeating the same one." We both had a chuckle. She knew I was with her, not against her. I was making fun of our own music, which disarmed her instantly.

Playfulness and not taking yourself too seriously has the power to disarm most situations. Try it out. It is a subtle art, and it can work wonders.

Try putting a little reminder in your calendar every now and then to "not take yourself too seriously today!"

2. MAKE PEOPLE FEEL SPECIAL

People generally conspire for your success when you show up with playful energy. When you consciously go from thinking and feeling that the world and people are against you to a belief that people generally mean well, your energy will shift.

At the border crossing from Montenegro to Albania, we faced a huge line of cars. Sitting on my motorbike, wearing protective gear on a steaming hot day with sweat running down my face, I took my helmet off and started chatting to a family crammed in a car next to me. They even invited me to sit in their air-conditioned car. After a while (and with the queue hardly moving), the dad suggested we skip the long line and ride through the passengers-only line.

Thinking that border control might not be too excited about our line-skipping exercise, I consciously shifted my energy into playfulness, rather than an expectation to get busted. With a big smile and open heart, I rode past the cars and straight to the passenger line. I smiled at the customs guy, made a joke about being sweaty and hungry, and shared how excited I was to explore his country. He responded with a big smile back and waved us through without even checking our passports. Maybe he was just a nice guy anyway, but I was amazed how he responded with playfulness, and it felt like we were all in it together.

Every moment of humanity you have is the perfect moment to make someone feel special. It doesn't take more effort. All it takes is for you to show that they matter and that you care. Share a smile and be present in those brief moments with strangers.

Next time you are faced with a situation that could go either way, consciously shift your energy into playfulness. Make the other person genuinely feel special and watch more magic happen in your everyday experiences!

3. THAT SPARKLE IN YOUR EYES

Playfulness is reflected in your body language. A little smirk, a gentle nudge, a warm tone of voice, and open arms invite play. Oh, and that sparkle in your eyes. There is nothing more inviting than a mischievous twinkle in someone's eyes! It oozes charisma and playfulness. It invites others to step into playfulness with you.

Think of someone you admire for his or her playfulness. How do they hold themselves?

How would you speak and act if you were being playful? How can you invite playfulness through your body language?

4. A GENTLE INVITATION

Playfulness diffuses the pressure in human interactions. It helps you to courageously stand up for something or someone without being preachy, and it's a gentle invitation for others to follow you if they want to.

When you share your opinion and you know some people might disagree, do it in a way that does not make you sound superior to them. If you share your thoughts playfully, you will not only be able to connect with people who have completely different views, but you will also build trust very quickly and lead in a subtle way.

For example, you might engage in a political discussion with someone who has completely opposing views. Instead of putting them down and positioning your opinion above theirs, share your thoughts playfully. You both have had different experiences which brought you to your beliefs. Instead of closing down and imposing your opinions, a level of playfulness might lead to more enlightening conversations.

5. LIGHTHEARTEDLY SERIOUS

Playfulness allows you to be light-hearted even in the face of fears. This doesn't mean not taking a situation seriously. Playfulness brings a lighter shade to challenging situations. This is where the fine line lies between not taking something seriously and adding a scoop of lightheartedness to take the edge off.

There are different ways to add lightheartedness, and you will find what works best for you. And remember, it's all about the intentions behind your behavior. One way to bring lightheartedness to an interaction is to exaggerate.

Let's say you are out for dinner with a friend and he won't stop whining about the red wine being too cold. Rather than discounting him, playfully exaggerate by saying something like, "I know! Life is tough. We get to go for dinner together and someone is even cooking for us!" Or if your brother is constantly telling you how life is unfair, rather than brushing him off, you might playfully mention how, "It's so hard to live in this beautiful country where shelter, food, and clothing are taken care of! Imagine how much fun it would be if we had to go hunting for food every day and had no running water or electricity!" Exaggerate with a smirk and kindness, not cynicism. Instead of buying into certain behaviors or reacting to them, respond playfully. It's not about finger-pointing, but about disarming disempowering stories.

With my teams, we use a term called "issues *à la carte*." It's a playful way to embrace challenges. Whenever we are facing an obstacle, we've found that we have more success when we come at it with playful courage. It's a way for us to add playfulness to situations that can be a little frustrating and often outside of our control.

6. KEEP A CURIOUS MIND

Curiosity is such a great driver of playful courage. When you adopt a childlike curiosity and go through life with an open and curious mind, you will naturally feel pulled towards courage. Life will be filled with wonderment.

Children are such a great example of this. They aren't scared of looking closely at a bug, falling over, or asking a million questions. Their curious mind is playful. They continuously look at the world through a lens of wonder. Their playfulness leads them to be more courageous without second-guessing everything.

Ask more questions. Follow a crab on the beach. Explore your neighborhood. Mix up the ingredients when cooking your favorite meal. Invite your childlike curiosity to bring forth your playful side.

7. BE PLAYFULLY UNFUCKWITHABLE

Lastly, become unfuckwithable! When you are unfuckwithable, you have a slight touch of irreverence. You're at peace and in touch with yourself, and nothing anyone says about you bothers you. You do your thing. You don't buy into negativity or drama. How can you let fears dominate your life if you are unfuckwithable? You can't!

When you are playfully unfuckwithable, you are free of inhibiting societal rules that make no sense, and you step into courage instead. You will do what's right and do it your own way.

Do unfuckwithable playfully, not seriously or aggressively.

How can you be more playfully unfuckwithable? Where in your life are you following rules or guidelines that are holding you back from living boldly?

And most importantly, don't forget to have fun with playfulness. Fun is fun! Fun and playfulness are great company.

You can learn to be more playful through practice. And it doesn't take more time in your already busy schedule. It's a way of being, one that invites you to live boldly.

Let's play and put this principle to work!

TRAVEL TUNES

- I don't take myself too seriously.
- I have a curious mind.
- I am playfully unfuckwithable.

PIT STOP: NOT TAKING YOURSELF TOO SERIOUSLY

Write your very own issues à la carte as you observe challenges that appear often, then look at them with a playful attitude. A few ideas for your issues a la carte might include being stuck in traffic on your way to work, having a disagreement with your partner about the same thing over and over again, or forgetting to bring your lunch.

TRAVEL JOURNAL

It's time to stop, reflect, and ponder the following questions:

- How can you approach life with more playfulness? What would happen if you were more playful in your daily life?
- Where are you lacking playfulness?
- Who is someone playful you admire? What makes them playful?
- If you approached life in a more playful way, what brave decisions would you make?
- How would you show up differently if you were to embrace playfulness?
- What is something you used to love but stopped doing? How can you invite more play into your life?

PRINCIPLE 12: EVOLUTION

Evolution is an important part of the human experience; it pushes boundaries and allows humanity to achieve the extraordinary.

Evolution also pushes your courage boundaries and supports you in becoming the best person you can be in this lifetime. With evolution comes change, and with change comes uncertainty. It takes courage to evolve.

Step into courage and you will be more willing to leave your safe cocoon in order to rise to new levels. You will welcome evolution by putting yourself into situations where you know you will expand, despite feeling uncomfortable.

EXPAND YOUR COURAGE BOUNDARIES

As you embrace evolution, your courage boundaries will change. If you consciously choose to keep evolving, you will be more likely to keep pushing your courage boundaries, rather than letting them shrink. What once felt unsafe might start to feel safe, and your boundaries will continuously expand. Practice making courageous decisions and you will see that they become less scary. What may be frightening now will become normal!

Whenever you have two options—a safe one and one that gives you goosebumps—which one will you choose?

Athletes train to be their best even in the most difficult circumstances. Train to be courageous so that you are able to make bold decisions, especially when you are challenged or facing your biggest fears.

As you go through life, you often have to reinvent yourself multiple times. Evolution is an incredibly powerful tool to embrace as you reinvent yourself with courage. As you invest in your own growth and upgrade yourself, you will find that all levels of your life will follow on with that upgrade, including the people and opportunities you attract.

GET COMFORTABLE WITH THE UNCOMFORTABLE

Get uncomfortable! It takes courage to put yourself into situations that are outside your comfort zone. Yet it is exactly those moments that stretch you that will help you grow and become a more evolved and courageous version of yourself.

If you feel uncomfortable or nervous when faced with something new, welcome that feeling as a sign of growth. Every time you feel butterflies in your stomach (not the "I'm in love" ones but the "I'm frickin' scared!" ones), you are most likely evolving.

I love grabbing every opportunity I can find to put myself into that "butterfly state" so I don't become complacent and instead keep expanding my courage boundaries. I know that when my fear buttons are pushed, I'm growing.

You might not see the benefit of feeling uncomfortable at first. However, whenever you get a chance to metaphorically jump off a cliff that makes your legs feel weak and your heart race faster, say yes! Say yes to not staying safe. Yes to feeling the fear. Yes to taking action despite the fear. Yes to evolving into the best human you can be. Yes to expanding your courage boundaries. Yes to evolution.

Get comfortable with the uncomfortable! The more you put yourself into uncomfortable situations, the more comfortable you get with them.

Let me give you three ideas to help you get uncomfortable!

1. FACE THE DIFFICULT CONVERSATIONS

"Franziska, it's the courage to have the difficult conversations that makes life even richer," one of my dear friends once said. This thought has stayed with me ever since.

Where in your life do you need to be more courageous and address the conversations that are scaring you a little? Which conversations do you need to have in order to evolve and stay in your truth?

Is a team member not pulling his or her weight? Do you need to have a challenging conversation with a loved one? Or are you avoiding an honest conversation with yourself?

Get uncomfortable and grasp the courage to face the difficult discussions that help you (and others) evolve.

2. BREAK THINGS

Don't be scared to break things (metaphorically) in order to push them (and yourself) to evolve.

It's uncomfortable, but it takes courage to throw out the old and open the door for the new. Sometimes that is exactly what's needed in order to evolve and go to the next level. Are there any areas in your life you need to "break" so you can rebuild and elevate them?

Abandoning a plan takes courage. It can be incredibly scary and rewarding at the same time, and you often end up at an even better destination than you had imagined.

Fears may lead you to hold on to a plan with both of your hands, even if you can see it falling apart all around you. Courage will push you to let go when necessary or to adjust and course-correct along the way.

In my businesses, I sometimes purposefully break and pull apart a process or system in order to rebuild it stronger. I do believe that as a leader it is your job to continuously push for evolution and not to settle for mediocrity. Your leadership will inspire those around you to step up too.

It takes a lot of courage to let go of something good in order to achieve something great. Most people don't dare to evolve at that level because they're afraid of losing. If you believe that the universe always has your back, you know that making mistakes is part of your evolution.

So every now and then, why not take stock of your life? Get uncomfortable and ask yourself where you need to break something in order for the pieces to come back together even better.

3. EMBRACE CONTRAST

Get uncomfortable by putting yourself into contrasting and unfamiliar experiences. Contrast inspires creativity and expands your mind. Have you noticed that sometimes, when you find yourself in a situation that feels unfamiliar, you tap into more creativity?

Get uncomfortable and expand your courage boundaries by doing more of the things you normally wouldn't do. I love when a friend invites me to an activity I normally wouldn't be drawn to, even if my first reaction might be "I'm not really into that." If I haven't at least tried it once, I generally say yes.

I mentioned earlier that I recently went axe-throwing—not something I would normally get into, and it's highly unlikely I'll do it again. However, it turned out to be a fun night and I discovered that, despite my Swiss roots, I will not win any axe-throwing championships.

Contrast inspires creativity. Whether I'm roughing it with my adventure buddies, camping in the wilderness one day, or dressing up all fancy for a gala dinner the next, contrast helps me think differently. Contrasting situations feed your curious mind and invite new ideas.

Get uncomfortable by embracing contrast. Put yourself into different situations to expand your mind. This helps you to gain different perspectives and pushes you to evolve into the best human you can be.

THE FIVE LEVELS

There are five main levels you can choose to evolve in, both on your own or with loved ones.

You might choose to evolve in all five, or just focus on a few of these areas. You will naturally feel more drawn to some.

The five levels are your mental, emotional, physical, intellectual, and spiritual evolution. Let's go through them one by one and you can decide which ones to put on your Courage Map.

MENTAL EVOLUTION

Let's start with the mental evolution, because evolving your mindset is one of the most crucial steps when it comes to expanding your courage boundaries. Your mind is a powerful engine that will either support you in stepping into courage and achieving your highest dreams or allow fears to hold you back.

The good news is that your mind is very trainable and can become your best ally! I love doing mindset experiments to prove to myself how powerful the mind really is. One of my recent experiments was running the New York City marathon without training for it. I thought that if I leveraged my mind, running the 42.2-kilometer route would be a breeze. I thought this was a genius idea.

I underestimated the difficulty by a lot, and it was definitely not a breeze. However, my mind got me through running the whole thing, even when my body was ready to give up. I watched my self-talk and kept repeating, "I've got this" over and over again.

Every now and then, when my hips were sore or the blisters on my feet seemed unbearable, the little voice in my head would tempt me to give up by whispering, "Just get a yellow cab to the finish line, nobody would ever know!" I acknowledged the voice and responded, "Thank you, great idea, you clever thing, but I've got this!"

I made it to the finish line in just under five hours and got away without much damage . . . just sore ankles for about six months!

Feed your mind consciously with thoughts that help you to be more courageous in any area you choose. Make your mind your best ally in expanding your courage boundaries. Oh, and you don't need to run a marathon to prove that. In fact, I wouldn't recommend running a marathon without training.

Your mental evolution will influence the depth of the other four levels. The stronger your mind, the more you will achieve your desired level of evolution everywhere else. Stay aware of your thoughts and turn your mind into your strongest supporter throughout your journey.

EMOTIONAL EVOLUTION

Your emotional evolution supports you in having the courage to go deeper on an emotional level: to not be afraid of the depth, intensity, and range of emotions you experience. Learn from a rainbow of emotions without judging yourself or others.

Instead of avoiding emotions or pushing them down, you'll learn to be OK with tears running down your face when you feel hurt, being vulnerable with loved ones, feeling blissful in moments of serenity, and laughing so loud your neighbors can hear you.

Evolving emotionally also helps to develop your emotional intelligence and your ability to truly connect with others on an emotional level with compassion. The more you evolve emotionally, the more perceptive you'll be of someone else's emotions. You'll be able to notice more emotional subtleties and you'll be able to better respond with empathy, humanity, and kindness.

To advance your emotional evolution, observe how certain

situations or people make you feel—but don't judge them. Challenging circumstances are here to help you grow and evolve. With this openness to different kinds of feelings, with this invitation to feel a rainbow of emotions, you are more likely to approach life with courage.

When I set my intentions at the beginning of the year, I wrote down that I would like to go deeper on all five levels and I must say, I got more than I wished for on the emotional one. Sometimes I thought that the universe was playing a cosmic joke on me. And then I kept reminding myself that the darker emotions are also here to help me evolve and grow.

PHYSICAL EVOLUTION

Without your health, you have nothing. It doesn't matter how much money you have in the bank, or how many people love you. Without health, it's hard to enjoy anything else.

Your physical wellbeing also has a big impact on how you approach life every day.

Physical evolution is about looking after yourself so you can perform at your optimum. It includes exercise, eating well, and developing sleeping habits that support you. I'm not a health expert, so I won't tell you what to do, other than listen to your body (and consult experts who study this stuff). So many people are dependent on their devices to find out if they had a good night's sleep, if they are hungry, or if they need exercise. Biotech is incredible. However, it's not a substitute to listening to your body. So instead of only relying on your smartphone to assess your wellbeing, relearn how to tune in to your body. It will tell you what you need if you just pay attention.

Take care of yourself and you will be more likely to have the strength and clear mind to make bold decisions.

I remember when we rode our motorbikes along the "Highway to Hell" in Turkey, a road labelled the most dangerous in the world. I was pushed both mentally and physically. It's a dirt road winding up a steep mountain cliff, with switchback after narrow switchback. We were graced with rain and fog that day, which resulted in zero visibility, but that might have actually helped me to stay calm. since I couldn't see the steep drop-off on my right.

I was hugging the left wall tightly, gripping my handlebars so hard my knuckles turned white. The road took my breath away, literally. When we reached the top, I started breathing again. I felt exhausted both physically and mentally.

My riding limits had been pushed hard. I even managed to drop my bike twice without there really being any obstacle. My mind was making room for doubt and fears. Reading about the road and accidents that happen on it didn't help. I had to consciously keep reminding myself to stay focused on my abilities. My boundaries were pushed and expanded the further we traveled.

Push yourself a little bit every now and then and invest in your physical evolution. It will help you to come at life with courage.

INTELLECTUAL EVOLUTION

I'm a bit of a nerd, so this one gets me very excited. Your intellectual evolution is about feeding your inner geek with insights and information to support you in making brave decisions.

Evolving intellectually gives you the ability to have deeper discussions that push your boundaries. Dare to have an opinion. Dare to disagree gracefully. Dare to challenge and be challenged intellectually. I secretly love it when my loved ones question my thinking, because it helps me to rethink and evolve intellectually. And I absolutely adore geeky, mind-expanding conversations.

Feed your intellect. There are so many different ways to do so, such as reading, listening to podcasts, attending courses, geeking out with friends, or solving puzzles. Find what works for you. One of my best friends used to walk around with an encyclopedia when we were in high school and I must say her vocabulary was, and still is, very impressive!

SPIRITUAL EVOLUTION

Lastly, but not least importantly, let's delve into your spiritual evolution. You don't need to believe in aliens to evolve spiritually. Your spiritual evolution will help you trust and feel a sense of connection to something bigger than yourself.

Evolving spiritually will help you make brave decisions from your intuition. And while some of your intuitive decisions may seem irrational, they can be powerful. It takes courage to take action or make decisions that don't make sense logically. Yet it is often those bold decisions that have the biggest impact.

To evolve spiritually, you don't need to live in a cave and meditate for years. You might choose to tap into consciousness through a ten-minute daily meditation, the occasional contemplation, an immersion into nature, or any other practice that works for you.

Spiritual evolution may also include experiences you can't explain with logic. You might choose to explore new dimensions of life you're not familiar with. It takes courage to let go of the familiar and dive into the unknown. When you do, you might just be surprised by the magic you find!

Choose the level of evolution you feel pulled to work on most and get started.

The five levels of evolution can also be applied to the evolution of your relationships. Different relationships will support you in evolving on different levels.

THE EVOLUTION OF RELATIONSHIPS

As you evolve and get closer to your truest self, you will see all of your relationships evolve. Some will disappear, while others will level up with you.

Relationships are the spice of life. When you have the courage to go deep on some or all of the five levels with your loved ones, you will feel an even deeper sense of connection. With most friends, you are likely to cover one or two of the five levels. You might have a friend with whom you explore intellectual evolution by geeking out together, someone else who joins you on a spiritual journey, and someone who pushes you mentally. Relationships are such a great way to explore and evolve into the best human you can be—if you have the courage to go deeper.

In a romantic relationship, you might choose to go deep on all of the five levels. If you find someone who wants to explore all five with you, it's pretty special.

MASCULINE AND FEMININE ENERGY

It was a rainy night when Mike and I arrived drenched at a hotel on the Black Sea. I jumped in the hot shower, put on dry clothes, and asked the night guard in the lobby where we could find some live music. "Babylon," he said, pointing down the street.

Mike and I ended up at this quirky Turkish nightclub. A live band was playing some really interesting electronic rock mixed with Arabic sounds that made me feel like I was a character in an Arabian Nights tale. I was lost in the music when Mike asked, "What does music mean to you?" Such a great question. "Hmm, let me think for a minute," I responded, sipping some surprisingly delicious Turkish wine.

A song is usually made up of various parts and different instruments, each elevating the others to create a union of sounds. Each instrument is beautiful on its own (except for the clarinet or the bagpipe) but when they come together, the song is elevated. That's how I observe evolved relationships. We are whole on our own. But when two humans come together to play, when they have the courage to drop their guards and go deeper, magic happens.

For me, a song is the perfect analogy for a great romantic relationship. I see the bass in a song as the masculine energy, providing a solid foundation, carrying the melodies, and allowing for the harmonies to dance to the same beat.

The melodies are the feminine energy, blooming and thriving thanks to the drums and the bass. The masculine energy is the fertile ground for the feminine energy to sprout, and together they evolve the relationship.

Masculine and feminine energies can be manifested in both men and women.

This is why comments like "my better half" or "my other half" don't make sense. You are not a half; you are whole. When two wholes come together, when the bass and the melody play in harmony, it creates a powerful union. They magnify each other's potentials, helping both people evolve into the best humans they can be.

It takes courage to be with someone courageous, because neither of you "need" each other—you choose each other. It's great to have someone who is equally willing to drop all the layers and go deep on some or all of the five levels. Courage allows you to dive deep in order for both of you to elevate.

Love boldly and you won't need to play games, because there is nothing to lose. You know and communicate what you want, hold on to your truth, and stand up for what you believe in. You give and receive without expectations. You grow together and you push each other to reach new levels.

Every relationship is an opportunity to learn and evolve. Let evolution support you in expanding your courage boundaries.

TRAVEL TUNES

- I am becoming a better human every day.
- I welcome feeling uncomfortable in order to evolve.
- I invest in myself.

PIT STOP: WELCOMING UNCOMFORTABLE

Get used to facing challenges courageously by getting comfortable with the uncomfortable. In the next thirty days, face up to at least one difficult conversation you know you must have. Say yes to experiences that make you feel uncomfortable.

TRAVEL JOURNAL

Grab your journal and ponder the following questions.

- How can you get uncomfortable in order to expand your courage boundaries?
- Which difficult conversation have you been putting off, even though you know it must be had in order to evolve?
- Which one of the five levels do you want to go deeper on? What actions will you take to evolve?
- Where do you feel stuck? What needs to happen for you to elevate?
- How can you evolve your relationships so they are based on courage instead of fear?

PRINCIPLE 13: COMMITMENT

You've made it to the last principle to support you in living boldly. Along the way, you've designed your Courage Map by pondering important questions and listening to supportive travel tunes. This is your guide to keep expanding your courage boundaries. You've put in some seriously awesome effort and it's almost time to celebrate! But first, let's lock it all in with the last principle: commitment.

COMMIT TO COURAGE

Each of the thirteen principles starts with an intention followed by action in order to expand your courage boundaries. Humming the travel tunes and pondering the pit stop questions are all part of the journey. Courage is a skill; the more you practice courage, the more courageous you become. You've already said yes to living boldly, now let's take that commitment to the next level.

Let's craft your commitment plan by going through the four stages outlined below.

1. IDENTIFY YOUR GOALS

Get clear on where you're currently at with your courage skills. Where in your life would you like to have more courage? While designing your Courage Map, you may have uncovered different areas you know you want to explore more.

Do you wish you had the courage to invest in a course to advance your career? Or leave a relationship that doesn't allow you to live in your truth? Or say yes to a crazy adventure? Or face a challenging conversation? Or sing in front of people? Or change careers? Or join a kick-boxing class and become the healthiest you have ever been? Or go skinny dipping?

Think about specific areas where you wish you had more courage. Make a list of anything that comes to mind.

2. TAKE YOUR PICK

There might be different areas of your life where you'd like to grow your courage boundaries. Rather than trying to be more courageous in every area of your life, pick one or two and focus.

Instead of attempting to adopt every single principle in this book at the same time, choose one and consciously embrace it until it becomes second nature. Once you've created a new habit, move to the next one. Prioritize as you see fit. And most importantly, have fun while you commit to practicing your new skills.

There will be times when your commitment levels will be tested. You may feel like giving up and defaulting back to staying safe or allowing fears to drive your actions. That's normal. Obstacles and challenges are here to test your commitment to yourself. Don't fight them or beat yourself up over your progress. Remember to flow.

For example, with the principle of non-attachment, you might struggle to detach from outcomes and let events influence your emotional state. That's ok. Progress often comes from tiny actions, so commit to taking small steps and trust in the process.

Don't expect overnight success. Consistent action will get you lucky!

3. GET LUCKY

The more you put the principles into action, the luckier you will get. Once you have clarity on where you want to be more courageous, commit to taking bold action in that direction and stay consistent. Consistency is important, and so is patience!

Patience is a virtue (I admit, it's not mine! But I'm getting better at it as the universe continues to test my patience). Staying committed to courage includes being patient enough to take consistent action despite difficulties or a delay in gratification.

As with a lot of worthy projects, your Courage Map might take time to design and implement. There is no rush. Let go of control, be adaptable, and be consistent.

And if you feel fears arise when taking action, don't worry—courage is about taking imperfect action despite the fear. Take more action and course-correct along the way.

4. ZIGZAG AND COURSE-CORRECT

Every now and then you might get pulled off course. Life is not a straight line; it is a zigzag with many twists and turns. It's the darkness and the light, the twists and the turns, the zig and the zag, that make it whole and rich. Life is a beautiful (and sometimes painful) dance between light and darkness.

There may be times when you choose to persevere gracefully and others when you choose to change direction. Have the awareness, flexibility, and courage to adjust your direction. When fear is driving your decisions, you may be more resistant to the unknown and stay stuck. When you choose to live boldly, you welcome change because you know everything is impermanent.

Course-correct with grace rather than force. Gracefulness is powered by courage, playfulness, and detachment. It's the courage to be OK with whatever happens. As long as you commit to staying true to yourself, you will act with dignity and integrity.

The universe often has its own way of working things out naturally. Staying in your courage allows you to embrace the unknown and adapt to the course-corrections that bring you and others to an even higher level.

PLAY BIG

I invite you to play a bigger game!

You are reading this book because you want to live more courageously. You are here because you have committed to yourself. You want to give life your best shot. You may even be here because you are ready to play a bigger game.

Your "big" will be different from someone else's, so don't worry about what anyone else is saying or doing. You are committing to your own dreams and goals.

A great way to check if you are dreaming courageously or staying safe is to see how you feel when you think about your dreams. Are you feeling butterflies in your stomach or any other sensation that reminds you of fear? Do you feel a deep sense of purpose? Do your dreams energize you? If so, perfect! And then maybe even go a little bigger. Go big enough so that you are stretching your courage boundaries and feeling a little bit uncomfortable, but not so big that you don't believe you can achieve those dreams.

Playing a bigger game can be daunting because it often comes with choices to shake things up and not stay safe. This shift can be scary. That's why a lot of people prefer to stay exactly where they are within the comfortable and familiar. And there is absolutely nothing wrong with that. However, if you commit to the bigger game of living courageously, you know that there will be uncertainties and unpredictability along the way. But you also know that the feeling of following your truth is priceless.

By playing a bigger game, you will inspire others to step up as well. It can be incredibly rewarding to see people around you step up and show up with an open heart.

Where in your life do you feel like you are thinking too small? Where are you playing safe? Where are you not committing to your truth? Where do you want to step up? What if you embarked on this crazy adventure you've always wanted to have? What if you asked the person you think is "out of your league" out on a date? What if you committed to staying true to yourself even when it's easier not to? What if you reached for the impossible?

IMPOSSIBLE IS AN OPINION

Don't you just cringe when somebody tells you that something is not possible? Maybe it's not possible in their world. However, maybe it is possible with your commitment to pushing your courage boundaries. Don't see impossible as an excuse to not take bold action. Impossible is an opinion, and it doesn't have to be yours.

Commit to courage and see "impossible" as a challenge. Remember, everything is impermanent, including impossible. What you may not be able to do now might be possible tomorrow. On your journey to courage, you will come across people and situations that will test your courage boundaries. Don't buy into impossible. Define your own possible and keep committing to living boldly. You've got this!

REMEMBER, IT'S NOT MOMMY'S FAULT

One of my wise friends once said, "Parents have your back, but you have to grow your own backbone." Your parents did the best they could with what they had at the time. And they most likely made mistakes. Commit to owning your results. Blaming someone else is giving your power away and most likely won't lead to a bold pursuit of your dreams.

We all have difficult experiences throughout life. But only you get to choose what they mean and which ones you carry with you. Don't blame mom, dad, the weather, or the economy for your problems. They may well have a huge impact on where you are now, but only you get to choose how you move forward. We all learn to pick up a victim story here and there based in fear. When that happens, change your story and recommit to yourself.

Commit to showing up in the world. Commit to showing up for yourself, because you deserve to live a courageous life. What happened in the past can't be undone. How you show up and act right now is your choice. Choose wisely.

LEAD WITH COURAGE

Your commitment to courage, and to the subtle shifts toward expanding your courage boundaries, will inspire those around you to also step up.

Whether you are leading a team, your family, or friends, you are first and foremost a leader of yourself. The better you get at leading yourself, the better you will be able to lead and inspire others—by walking the walk.

Think of the leaders you find most inspiring. What do they have in common? It's very likely that they are owning their truth, firmly standing by their principles, and evolving as they go. They lead with an open heart, playfulness, and pure intentions. They trust in themselves and in the process, embrace their imperfections, and remain incredibly adaptable. A courageous leader is someone who can lead with kindness, compassion, and empathy.

All the principles in this book will lead you to live a life with more courage, but they will also help you become a strong leader of yourself and others.

Commit to being courageous, standing in your truth, and doing so with grace, integrity, and dignity. Lead yourself and others with courage. Thank you for committing to yourself and showing up to the world courageously.

TRAVEL TUNES

- I am committed to living courageously.
- Impossible is an opinion.
- I embrace the zigzag of life.

PIT STOP: MAKING A COMMITMENT TO YOURSELF

Commit to courage every single day for the next thirty days. Every day you are faced with choices—rather than going the easy route, consciously pick the most courageous one.

TRAVEL JOURNAL

Grab your journal and write down your thoughts on the following questions.

- What is the next step you can take to bring you closer to courage?
- What are you willing to commit to right now to live your truth?
- Where have you avoided commitment to yourself or others because of your fears?
- Where have you not been owning up to your results? If you owned up, what would you change?
- How can you show up as the best leader of yourself and others?
- Where in your life do you want to play a bigger game? Where have you been playing small?

THE BEGINNING

You've begun your process of designing and improving your Courage Map, a guide that will support you on your journey through life. Every bold decision you make and every courageous action you take will bring you closer to living your best life.

Courage will lead you to a rich life without regrets, one you can truly be proud of. A life lived with courage is a wonderful, fulfilling, and memorable journey. You will look back on your courageous life with a full heart, knowing that you have given it your all. You have taken chances, you have failed, you have gotten back up, and you have lived all out.

Like with any journey, as your circumstances change and as you expand your courage boundaries, you will keep adjusting your map to support you. Whenever you get lost, need a courage injection, feel like you need a pit stop to refuel, or want to listen to new travel tunes to enhance your experience, come back to this book and your journal for ideas and guidance. Creating and following your Courage Map is a lifelong project.

Every day is a new chance to be courageous. Every day you get to choose how you want to show up. Some days you might feel more courageous than others. On some days you will flow effortlessly, while on others you will encounter difficult roadblocks. Trust that you are equipped with the tools you need to navigate around them. Remember, there are many different roads that lead to your destination. And sometimes a little unexpected detour brings you to some of the most beautiful places in life. Trust that the universe always has your back, even when you find yourself in a dark corner.

Remember that you are the author of your own stories. Own your truth, have pure intentions, trust in yourself, show up with an open heart, always respond with kindness, embrace your imperfections, detach from the outcome, surrender to flow, bring an attitude of playfulness, keep evolving, and commit! The world needs you and your gifts. And you deserve to live a courageous life.

Here's another quote from Steve Jobs that I love: "You can't connect the dots looking forward; you can only connect them looking backwards. So you have to trust that the dots will somehow connect in your future. You have to trust in something—your gut, destiny, life, karma, whatever. This approach has never let me down, and it has made all the difference in my life."

Each principle is a dot on your courage map. Trust that the dots will connect. You are doing the work, you are taking action, you are shaking things up, and you are being courageous. You are exactly where you are meant to be. The universe always has your back.

We are all in this together and I'm excited to hear about your experiences as you design and live your Courage Map. Enjoy your ride filled with an abundance of courageous moments!

A LOVE LETTER FROM COURAGE

Dear courageous soul,

It's me, your courage. I wanted to let you know that I'm always in your corner, even when you can't see me. Know that I'm never far away, even when you feel fear. I've always got your back.

You are a courageous soul—you always have been and you always will be. You are destined to boldly live your truth.

Thank you for trusting yourself and believing in me. We are a great team! Together we are unstoppable.

Here's to living boldly!

Yours truly,

Courage

ABOUT THE AUTHOR

Franziska is a maverick entrepreneur, leading marketing and brand strategist, adventurer, author and the co-founder of Basic Bananas, The Business Hood, Oceanlovers and Moments of Humanity.

In 2013 Franziska was awarded the Young Entrepreneur of the Year award recognizing her innovation, creativity and philanthropic involvement.

Franziska is a board member at the global Entrepreneurs Organization EO where she is advising on communications, marketing and branding. She also launched an impact initiative called EOcean to inspire entrepreneurs to be more sustainable.

Franziska sits on the judging panel for Singularity University and has run think tanks at the United Nations to address the UN sustainable development goals through entrepreneurship.

CONNECT WITH FRANZISKA ISELI

Sign up for Franziska's newsletter at
www.franziskaiseli.com/thecouragemap

To find out more information visit his website:
www.franziskaiseli.com

Facebook:
www.facebook.com/franziska.iseli.1

BOOK DISCOUNTS AND SPECIAL DEALS

CPSIA information can be obtained
at www.ICGtesting.com
Printed in the USA
FSHW022350070420
68925FS

9 781631 610813